PAUL SELIGSON
LEANNE GRAY
RICARDO SILI

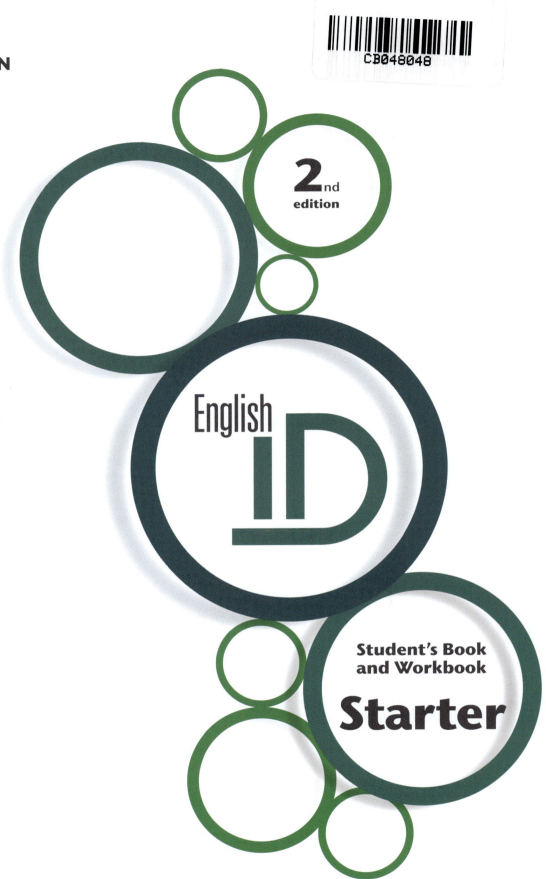

English ID

2nd edition

Student's Book and Workbook

Starter

ID Language map - Student's Book

	Question syllabus	Vocabulary	Grammar	Speaking & Skills
1	1.1 What's your name?	Opening greetings Numbers 1–12		Introduce yourself Say numbers
	1.2 Where are you from?	Classroom language		Introduce a friend
	1.3 What's this in English?	Classroom items Familiar items	*a* and *an* Verb *be* ⊕ ⊖ Contractions: *you're, it's, isn't, what's*	Name items in English
	1.4 What's your phone number?	The alphabet	Verb *be* ❓	Spell names Ask for & give personal information
	1.5 What's your email address?	Cognates Email		Recognize cognates
	How are you today?	Greetings		Complete a personal information form
	Writing 1: An introduction to an online group	**ID Café 1:** First class		
2	2.1 Are you a student?	Countries and nationalities Numbers 13–20 and plurals	I am / you are ⊕ ⊖ and personal pronouns	Ask & answer about people Say numbers & plural items
	2.2 Who's your favorite actor?	Opinion adjectives	*he / she / it is* ⊕ ⊖ Contractions	Talk about preferences Do a quiz about people & nationalities Ask for and express opinions about favorite people & things
	2.3 Is ceviche Mexican?	Numbers 20–100+	*Is he / she / it* ❓	Express opinions Say numbers & plural items Talk about age & years
	2.4 Where are your two favorite places?	Adjectives	*you / we / they are* ⊕ ⊖ ❓ Contractions	Write an online chat about a vacation
	2.5 Is English essential for your future?	Cognates		Read for general comprehension Complete a form about a classmate
	How old is Ariana Grande?			Share information about other people
	Writing 2: A blog post	**ID Café 2:** People, places, passports!		**Review 1** p.30
3	3.1 What do you do?	Jobs Job suffixes	*a* and *an* + jobs Plurals	Ask & answer about jobs
	3.2 Do you have brothers and sisters?	Family	Simple present: *I / you / we / they* ⊕ ⊖ ❓ Possessive adjectives	Talk about family
	3.3 Do you have a job?	Places of work	Simple present ❓	Ask & answer about jobs & places of work
	3.4 Where does your mother work?		Simple present: *he / she / it* ⊕ ⊖ ❓	Ask & answer about family
	3.5 Do you live near here?			Listen for specific information
	Where do you study?			Exchange personal information
	Writing 3: A personal profile	**ID Café 3:** Job interviews		
4	4.1 Is there an ATM near here?	Personal items Colors	*There + be*	Identify items
	4.2 Are those your books?		*this / that / these / those*	Say the names of personal items & colors
	4.3 What things do you lose?	Plural nouns Telling the time		Agree / Disagree with text Describe items & quantity
	4.4 What time do you get up?	Typical days	Simple present review	Ask & answer about your typical day
	4.5 How do you pronounce *meme* in English?	Information technology		Pronounce & spell cognates
	What color is your wallet?			Ask about lost property
	Writing 4: A description	**ID Café 4:** In the bag		**Review 2** p.56
5	5.1 Do you drink a lot of coffee?	Meals, food and drinks		Express opinions about food & drinks Talk about eating habits
	5.2 What's your favorite food?	Food	*like / love / don't like / hate*	Make a list of food & drinks Talk about things you like / don't like
	5.3 What do you usually do on Friday evenings?	Days of the week Weekend and free-time activities	Frequency adverbs	Ask & answer about, & compare weekend activities
	5.4 Do you like Rihanna's music?		Possessive 's Object pronouns	Guess classmates' possessions Ask for & share opinions about celebrities and brands
	5.5 Do you eat a lot of fast food?	Fast food		Notice sound–spelling combinations
	Anything to drink?	Opposites		Order food
	Writing 5: A reply to a social media post	**ID Café 5:** It's about taste		**Review 3** p.70

Grammar p. 72   Sounds and usual spellings p. 82   Audioscript p. 84

ID Language map - **Workbook**

	Question syllabus	Vocabulary	Grammar	Speaking & Skills
1 1.1	What's your name?	Opening greetings Numbers 1-12		Introduce yourself Write numbers
1.2	Where are you from?	Classroom language		Ask & answer personal questions
1.3	What's this in English?	Classroom items Familiar items	*a* and *an* Verb *be* ➕ ➖ Contractions: *you're, it's, isn't, what's*	Name items in English
1.4	What's your phone number?	The alphabet	Verb *be* ❓	Write your profile
1.5	What's your email address?			Complete a form
2 2.1	Are you a student?	Countries and nationalities Numbers 13–20	*I am / you are* ➕ ➖	Ask & answer about people
2.2	Who's your favorite actor?	Opinion adjectives	*he / she / it is* ➕ ➖ and personal pronouns Contractions	Express opinions
2.3	Is ceviche Mexican?	Numbers 20–100+	*Is he / she / it* ❓	Write numbers Do a quiz
2.4	Where are your two favourite places?		*you / we / they are* ➕ ➖ ❓ Contractions	Give personal information
2.5	Is English essential for your future?	Personal information		Share information about other people
3 3.1	What do you do?	Jobs	*a* and *an* + jobs Plurals	Ask & answer about jobs
3.2	Do you have brothers and sisters?	Family	Simple present: *I / you / we / they* ➕ ➖ Possessive adjectives	Ask & answer about family
3.3	Do you have a job?	Places of work	Simple present ❓	Complete a survey
3.4	Where does your mother work?		Simple present: *he / she / it* ➕ ➖ ❓	Read an email
3.5	Do you live near here?			Compare people's interests
4 4.1	Is there an ATM near here?	Personal items	There + *be*	Identify items
4.2	Are those your books?	Colors	*this / that / these / those*	Say the names of personal items
4.3	What things do you lose?	Plural nouns Telling the time	There + *be*	Identify items Tell the time
4.4	What time do you get up?	Typical days	Simple present review	Talk about a typical day
4.5	How do you pronounce *meme* in English?	Information technology		Read and talk about social networks
5 5.1	Do you drink a lot of coffee?	Meals, food and drinks		Talk about eating preferences
5.2	What's your favorite food?	Food	*like / love / don't like / hate*	Talk about eating habits
5.3	What do you usually do on Friday evenings?	Days of the week Weekend and free-time activities	Frequency adverbs	Talk about your week & weekend activities
5.4	Do you like Rihanna's music?		Possessive *'s* Object pronouns	Talk about famous people
5.5	Do you eat a lot of fast food?	Fast food		Read an email Talk about favorite food & drink

Audioscript p. 114   Answer Key p. 116   Phrase Bank p. 118   Word List p. 120

Welcome to English ID!

Finally, an English course you can understand!

Famous **song lines** illustrate language from lessons.

Lesson titles are questions to help you engage with the content.

Word stress in pink on new words.

Focus on **Common mistakes** accelerates accuracy.

ID Skills: extra reading and listening practice.

ID in Action: communication in common situations.

ID Café: sitcom videos to consolidate language.

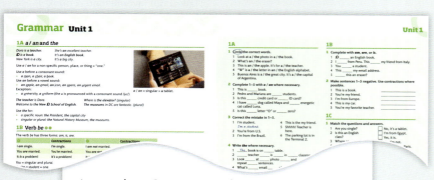

A complete **Grammar** reference with exercises.

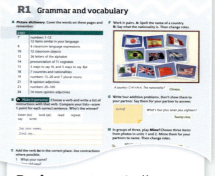

Reviews systematically recycle language.

Welcome

Contextualized Picture Dictionary to present and review vocabulary.

Stimulating **Grammar** practice.

Speech bubbles: models for speaking.

Make it personal: personalized speaking tasks to help you express your identity in English.

Audio script activities to consolidate pronunciation.

Pictures to present and practice **Pronunciation**.

Workbook to practice and consolidate lessons.

 Richmond *Learning* **Platform**

- Teachers and students can find all their resources in one place.
- **Richmond Test Manager** with interactive and printable tests.
- Activity types including pronunciation, common mistakes and speaking.

Phrase Bank to practice common expressions.

Learn to express your identity in English!

1

1.1 What's your name?

1 Listening

A ▶1.1 Listen and (circle) the correct words in the dialogue. Complete the teacher's ID card.

T Hello. **Wel**come to the New ID School of **En**glish. I'm Isadora, your **tea**cher / **stu**dent.
S Hi, Isadora.
T **What** / **What's** your name?
S My name is Luiza.
T Nice to meet you, Luiza.
S Nice to meet you too, Isadora.
T Please, call me **Isa**, / **Do**ra.

B ▶1.2 Listen and repeat. In pairs, practice with your names.

I'm Isadora. What's your name?   My name is Alejandro. Please, call me Alex.

C ▶1.3 Read the students' ID cards and complete the dialogue. Listen, check, and repeat. Practice with your names.

M Hello, I'm Mariana.
P Hi, _____.
M Please, call me Mari. What's your _____?
P My name is _____.
M Nice to meet _____, Pedro.
P _____ to _____ you too, Mari.

Common mistakes
I'm 's
I Pedro. What your name?

D Read the information and pronounce the pink-stressed words from the dialogue in **A**.

Word stress is **ve**ry im**por**tant for good pronunci**a**tion. In ID, **pink** **le**tters in**di**cate stress.

E 🎤 **Make it personal** Introduce yourself to your classmates. How many names do you remember?

Hello. / Hi. I'm ... (Please call me ...)   My name is ... Nice to meet you.

② Vocabulary Numbers 1-12

A ▶1.4 Listen to the song extract, then use the pictures to sing it. Write the numbers 1–12 next to the correct words.

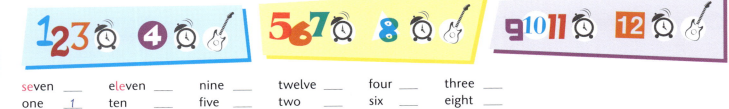

| seven ___ | eleven ___ | nine ___ | twelve ___ | four ___ | three ___ |
| one _1_ | ten ___ | five ___ | two ___ | six ___ | eight ___ |

B *Dictation!* In pairs, say five numbers for your partner to write. Then change roles.

Eight, three, eleven, two, nine.

C ▶1.5 Listen and say the number of the item you hear.

Bye bye.

Number four ... The hospital.

D 🔊 Make it personal In groups of three, race each other.
  A: Say a number or item.
  B and C: Race to say the correct answer. One point for the fastest each time.

1.2 Where are you from?

1 Vocabulary Classroom language

A ▶1.6 Listen to the teacher and complete instructions 1–6. Listen again and repeat.

read

listen to

look at

say

complete

repeat

1 _____ the exercise.
2 _____ the dialogue.
3 _____ the photos.
4 _____ the text.
5 _____ the words.
6 _____ the sentence.

> **Common mistakes**
>
> Listen ~~/~~ the teacher. *(to)*
> Look ~~/~~ the photos. *(at)*
> The is singular and plural.

B ▶1.7 Listen and follow the model. Practice the sentences.

> Listen to the dialogue. – The sentence.   Listen to the sentence.

C Do you know other classroom instructions? Make a list with your teacher.

> Open your book.   Work in pairs.

D 🔒 Make it personal Play *Mime*! Take turns miming a classroom instruction for the class to guess.

2 Listening

🎵 Listen to the Mariachi play at midnight
Are you with me, are you with me? **1.2**

A ▶1.8 Look at the photo and listen. What are the students' names? Where are they from?

Number 1 is ...

▶ Hi, Pedro!
▶ Hello, Mari. Good to see you.
▶ Yes, you _____. Pedro, this is my friend, Luiza.
▶ Nice to _____ you, Luiza.
▷ _____ to meet you too. Please call me Lu.
▶ OK, and where are you from, Lu? _____?
▷ No, I'm not. I'm from _____. And you?
▶ I'm from _____.

B ▶1.8 Listen again and complete the dialogue. Then, in groups of three, role-play.

C Match the sentence halves.

1 Dora, this ...
2 Hi, Fernanda! It's good ...
3 This is my ...
4 Hello, Dora. Nice ...
5 Where are ...
6 I'm ...

☐ ... to see you.
☐ ... is Paula.
☐ ... you from?
☐ ... from Guatemala City.
☐ ... teacher, Dora.
☐ ... to meet you.

Common mistakes

D ▶1.9 Listen and follow the model. Practice the sentences.

Where are you from? – Santiago.   *I'm from Santiago.*

E 🎤 **Make it personal** In groups of three, introduce one friend to the other. When your teacher says "change," form a different group of three and repeat. Do you know everyone's name now?

(Ana), this is my friend, (Fred).   *Nice ...*   *... you too.*   *Where ... you from?*   *I'm from ...*

1.3 What's this in English?

1 Vocabulary Classroom items

A Name five items you can see in your classroom – in English!

B ▶1.10 Match items 1–12 to the words. Listen, check, and repeat.

- [2] a book
- [ ] a chair
- [ ] a desk
- [ ] a flash drive
- [ ] an eraser
- [ ] an interactive whiteboard
- [ ] a marker
- [ ] a notebook
- [ ] an online dictionary
- [ ] a pen
- [ ] a pencil
- [ ] a tablet

C ▶1.11 Listen to Dora and Pedro. Check the four items they mention in **B**.

D ▶1.11 Listen again and complete the dialogue.
- Pedro Dora, what's this in English? Is it a pen?
- Dora No, it isn't. It's a _____.
- Pedro Ah, yes, thanks. And _____ this in English?
- Dora It's an _____. What's _____?
- Pedro I don't know.
- Dora Let's look in the _____.
- Pedro OK ... Ah, yes, it's a _____. Thanks.
- Dora You're _____.

Common mistakes

~~This is the book.~~ → This is *a* book.
It's
~~Is an apple.~~ → *It's* an apple.
~~Is a pencil?~~ → *Is it* a pencil?
~~No, is a pen.~~ → No, *it's* a pen.
~~I don't No know.~~ → I *don't* know.

2 Grammar *a* and *an*

A ▶1.12 Listen to and read the grammar box. Then complete 1–5 with *a* or *an*.

• Use **a** with consonant sounds.	• Use **an** with vowel sounds.
a book, a student, a teacher	an airport, an elephant, an ID card

→ Grammar 1A p. 72

1. A Macbook is _____ type of computer.
2. Write me _____ email.
3. Look, _____ Italian restaurant!
4. *La Traviata* is _____ opera.
5. This is _____ envelope.

B Cover the words in **1B**. In pairs, look at the photos and remember.

What's number 9?
It's an eraser.

C 🗣 **Make it personal** In pairs, test your partner's memory. Then change roles.
- A: Put some of the classroom items from **1B** on your desk.
- B: Look at the items for 10 seconds. Close your eyes and remember.

♪ Oh-oh, I'm an alien, I'm a legal alien, I'm an Englishman in New York.

1.3

3 Grammar   Verb *be* ➕ ➖

A ▶1.13 **Read the grammar box and complete dialogues 1–4 with *'m, are, is, 's* or *isn't*. Listen, check, and repeat.**

Questions ❓	Positive ➕	Negative ➖
Where **are** you from?	**I'm** from Lima.	**I'm not** from Arequipa.
	You're from Bogotá.	**You're not** from Baranquilla.
What**'s** this?	It**'s** a flash drive.	It**'s not** an eraser.
Are you a teacher?	Yes, I **am**.	No, **I'm not**.
Is it a tablet?	Yes, it **is**.	No, it **isn't**.

Contractions
you're = you are   it's = it is   isn't = is not   what's = what is

➡ **Grammar 1B** p. 72

Common mistakes
'm
I̶ from Santiago.
   it is
Yes, i̶t̶'̶s̶.

1. A Hello, José. Where _____ you from?
   B I _____ from Bogotá.

2. A What _____ this in English? _____ it a pen?
   B No, it _____ a pen. It _____ a marker.

3. A _____ you Dora, the teacher?
   B No, I _____ not. I _____ a student too.

4. A _____ you from Brazil?
   B Yes, I am. I _____ from Salvador.

Common mistakes
What
H̶o̶w̶ is this in English?
What
H̶o̶w̶ do you call this?

B ▶1.14 **Listen and follow the model. Practice the sentences.**

What's this in English? – A pen.   *It's a pen.*

C 🔊 **Make it personal** **Familiar items** In pairs, speculate about photos 1–10. Do you recognize all the items?

What's number 1? I don't know.
Is it a games console?
No, I think it's a computer mouse.
Oh, yes, you're right.

1.4 What's your phone number?

1 Pronunciation The alphabet

A **H J K 8**
___ **C D E G P T V Z 3**
___ **L M N S X 7**
___ **Y 5 9**
Q ___ **W 2**

A ▶ 1.15 Listen to and complete the doctor's chart. Which two letters of the alphabet are missing?

B ▶ 1.16 Listen to and repeat the letters.

C ▶ 1.17 Listen to and read the information. In pairs, say the alphabet in order.

> English has 26 letters: 21 consonants and five vowels, A, E, I, O and U. Memorize the letters in the five sound groups in the chart. Remember O and R too.

D Say these acronyms in English. Then in pairs, write one for your partner to say.

E 🎧 **Make it personal** Spelling tennis In groups of three, one person says a word and the other two spell the word with alternate letters.

Spell "door."   double o
       d   r

2 Listening

A ▶ 1.18 Listen and match parts 1 and 2 of the conversation to the pictures. Are Angela and Daniel classmates or friends?

♪ A B C, it's easy as 1 2 3,
As simple as do re mi,
A B C, 1 2 3
Baby you and me girl.

1.4

B ▶1.19 Match questions 1–6 to the answers. Listen, check, and repeat.

1 Are you in my English class?
2 How are you?
3 What's your phone number?
4 What's your name?
5 Can you spell that, please?
6 Are you on WhatsApp?

☐ It's 78190366.
☐ O-C-H-O-A. It's a Mexican name.
☐ Yes, I am. Message me.
☐ It's Angela Ochoa.
☐ I'm fine, thanks.
☐ At the New ID school of English? Yes, I am.

C Read the information.
A: Spell a name from the Contact list.
B: Say the person's phone number.

In phone numbers:
0 (zero) = oh
66 = double 6
007 = double oh seven

In names:
LL = double L
In acronyms:
BBC = B-B-C (not double B-C)

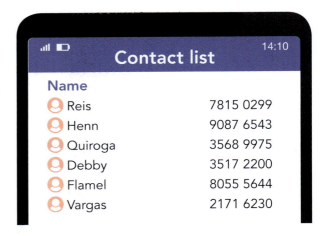

R-E-I-S.   7-8-1-5-oh-2-double 9.

D 😊 Make it personal 📡 Search online for some useful numbers. In pairs, dictate them to your partner.

The local hospital is 419 228 3385.

③ Grammar Verb *be* ❓

A ▶1.20 Put the words in 1–7 in order to make questions. Then match them to the answers. Listen and check. In pairs, practice.

1 's / in / what / this / English / ?
  What's this in English?
2 you / married / are / ?
3 you / today / how / are / ?
4 name / your / what / 's / ?
5 from / where / you / are / ?
6 phone / 's / your / what / number / ?
7 cell / where / my / 's / phone / ?

➡ **Grammar 1C** p.72

☐ No, I'm single.
☐ Paulo.
☐ It's an eraser.
☐ It's on the table.
☐ I'm from Córdoba.
☐ It's 631… er, sorry, I don't remember.
☐ I'm OK, thanks.

⚠ **Common mistake**
Are you
~~You are~~ married?

B ▶1.21 Listen and follow the model. Practice the sentences.

2274 3690 – Question.   *What's your phone number?*

C 😊 Make it personal In groups of three, ask questions to complete the table.

Name	Phone number	Hometown

What's your name?
What's your phone number?
Where are you from?

1.5 What's your email address?

ID Skills Recognizing cognates

A What do these words have in common? Check your answer at the bottom of page 15.

alphabet   bar   dialogue   experience   interesting   restaurant
complete   dictionary   identity   plural   vocabulary

B Read the blogs. Who likes English more, wallyjoe or Roxanne? Underline the cognates in the blogs and guess the pronunciation.

Bloggers ❤ English

English is an incredible language. It's flexible and receptive. English is, in effect, a collection of languages. About 60% of its vocabulary is Latin-based!

(posted by wallyjoe on www.mylot.com)

English is an incredible language. I adore it! There's a perfect word or expression for anything a person can imagine. For example, 'adore'… It's a splendid word! It transcends 'love.' It contains respect, devotion, and a sense of eternity. Wow …

(posted by Roxanne on urthmthr.blogspot.com.br)

C ▶ 1.22 Reread and listen to the blogs to check. Circle the words you don't understand. In pairs, compare. Any surprises?

D In pairs, find 10 more cognates in Unit 1. What other English words or phrases do you know?

> I love you.   Pop music.   Made in China.

E ▶ 1.23 Listen and complete the form.

Name: _____
City / country: _____, Brazil
Email: _____.ch@_____.com
Phone number: _____

F ▶ 1.24 Listen to, read, and repeat the words. Then say email addresses 1–3.

@ = at   . = dot   - = hyphen   _ = underscore   # = hashtag
Spell combinations of letters, for example, .ar, .mx.
Pronounce .com, .co, .org, .net as words.

1 email.account1234@portmail.com.mx
2 josy_turner@cpg.net
3 always-smiling@fishers.org.us

G 🔒 Make it personal What's your email address in English? Say it to the class and make a class email list.

14

How are you today?

♪ *Baby, we don't stand a chance,
It's sad but it's true
I'm way too good at goodbyes.*

1.5

1

2

> ⚠️ **Common mistake**
>
> *evening*
> Hello, good ~~night~~!
> Use *Good night* to say goodbye after 6 p.m.

ID in Action Greetings and personal information

A ▶1.25 Match photos 1 and 2 to groups A and B. Then listen to and repeat the phrases.

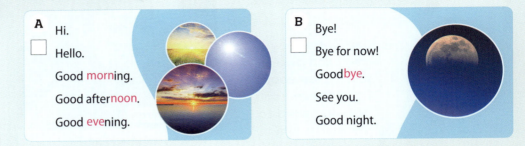

A ☐
- Hi.
- Hello.
- Good **morn**ing.
- Good after**noon**.
- Good **eve**ning.

B ☐
- Bye!
- Bye for now!
- Good**bye**.
- See you.
- Good night.

B ▶1.26 Listen to three conversations. Check the expressions in **A** that you hear.

C ▶1.26 Listen again and match pictures a–c to conversations 1–3.

 a ☐

 b ☐

 c ☐

D ▶1.27 Complete 1–7 with these words. Listen, check, and repeat.

| are (x2) | email | Good | See | What's (x2) | you | your |

1 How ___are___ you?
2 _____ your name?
3 Bye! _____ you!
4 What's your _____ address?
5 Where _____ _____ from?
6 Hello! _____ evening!
7 _____ _____ phone number?

E 🎤 **Make it personal** In pairs, say hello and ask questions to complete the form.

Name: _____   Address: _____
Hometown: _____   Phone number: _____
Email: _____   Vehicle regist**ra**tion number: _____
ID card number: _____

> Good afternoon. How are you today?

> Hello, I'm fine, thanks. And you?

> I'm fine. What's your name?

> I'm …

Answer: They are all **cog**nates. A cognate is a word **sim**ilar in **o**rigin to your language.

15

Writing 1   An online introduction

♪ *Beautiful people,
Drop top, designer clothes,
Front row at fashion shows.*

A ◯ 1.28 Read the posts in this social network group and complete the forms for the two new members.

Welcome new members!

To start: intro**duce** yourself and give us your o**pin**ion about a **fa**vorite ce**leb**rity. Use one word to des**cribe** him or her!

Ana Belle

Aysel Evren

<mark>Nice to meet you all.</mark> My name's Aysel Evren. I'm Turkish, from Izmir. I'm 17 years old, I'm a student, and I'm single. Ed Sheeran's my favorite musician. I think he's fan**tas**tic.

Ale Benítez

<mark>Hi, ev**ery**one.</mark> I'm Alejandro Benítez, but please call me Ale. I'm from Guadalajara, Mexico, I'm a chef, and I'm 24. I'm married. My favorite celebrity's Jennifer Lawrence. I think she's an **ex**cellent **ac**tor.

Profile

1	Name	Aysel Evren	Alejandro _____
2	Nickname		
3	City / Country (nationality)	Izmir, Turkey (Turkish)	
4	Age		
5	**Ma**rital status		
6	Favorite celebrity		Jennifer Lawrence
7	Opinion word		

B Match 1–7 in **A** to these questions.
- ☐ Where are you from?
- ☐ What's your name?
- ☐ Are you married?
- ☐ What's your nickname?
- ☐ How old are you?
- ☐ Who's your favorite celebrity?
- ☐ What's your opinion of him / her?

C Reread the posts and write down the sentences that mean 1–4.
1. I'm from Turkey. = I'm _____
2. I'm not married. = _____
3. I'm Mexican, from Guadalajara. = _____
4. I'm 24 years old. = _____

D Read *Write it right!* and (circle)...
- 14 contractions
- six commas
- three uses of *and*
- one use of *but*

✓ **Write it right!**

Use contractions ('m, 's, 're) in posts.
Use a comma (,), *and*, or *but* to connect two ideas.

E *Your turn!* Write a post to the group.

Before	Answer the questions in **B** and complete your profile.
While	Use a <mark>highlighted</mark> phrase to say hello to the group. Check your use of *and*, *but*, and commas.
After	"Post" your texts around the class. Any coincidences?

1 First class

 Café

1 Before watching

A Match the opposites. Then test a partner.

1 beautiful — last
2 first — Slow down!
3 here — thanks
4 Hurry up! — energetic
5 an instructor — early
6 late — finish
7 please — there
8 start — a student
9 this — ugly
10 tired — that

What's the opposite of tired?   *Energetic. What's ...*

B Look at the picture. Where are they?

- in a gym
- in an apartment
- in a classroom
- in a theater

2 While watching

A Watch until 0:44 and complete extracts 1–3.

1 **Jim** Could you spell that for me, please?
  Andrea Sure. __ - A - I - N - __ - __ - I - G - H - T.
2 **Jim** What's your _____?
  Andrea Andrea.
  Jim Great. OK, __ __, please?
3 **Jim** Could you spell your last name, please?
  Lucy __ - E - __ - E - __ - __ - A   __ - A - R - __ - I - __.

B ⬤ Make it personal In pairs, spell your name. Then each invent another name and ask and answer.

What's your name, please?   *Salceda. That's S - A - L - C - E - D - A.*

C Watch the complete video. True (T) or false (F)?

1 The instructor's name is Jim Landry.
2 It's a beginner class.
3 The yoga class is in Room 2.
4 August isn't in the yoga class.
5 Daniel's in the capoeira class.
6 August is on the class list.
7 The class isn't very good.

D Complete the extract. Watch from 2:12 to 2:45 again to check.

Daniel: Uh, _____ this Room 2?
Instructor: No. Room 2 _____ next door.
August: Oh. Sorry. What _____ is this?
Andrea: August? _____ you in our _____ class?
August: Yoga? Yes. Actually, yes, I _____.
Daniel: Huh? August, we _____ in the capoeira _____.
August: No, no ... You'_____ in capoeira. I _____ in the _____ class!

3 After watching

A Complete 1–8 with August (Au), Andrea (An), the instructor (I), Daniel (D), or Lucy (Lu).

1 _____ is in line first.
2 _____ arrives late and brings coffee.
3 _____ says, "It's so early!"
4 _____ signs her name on _____'s list first.
5 _____ says, "The yoga class starts at 8:30."
6 _____ and _____ have the same last name.
7 _____ goes to the capoeira class.
8 _____ thinks the first class is great.

B Check the category for phrases 1–9: greeting or goodbye (GOG), introducing yourself (IY), or asking for information (AFI).

		GOG	IY	AFI
1	Hey, Lucy!			
2	Good morning.			
3	I'm Jim Landry!			
4	Could you spell your name?			
5	ID, please?			
6	You can call me Lucy.			
7	Hello, everyone!			
8	Is this room 2?			
9	See you later!			

C ⬤ Make it personal *Role-play!* In groups of three, **A**: You're the instructor. **B** and **C**: You're in the class. Use the phrases in **B**. Introduce yourself, give information and say goodbye to your partners. Change roles.

Hello, I'm Sam. Is this the yoga class?   *Hi, yes, it is. I'm the instructor. My name's Juan Carlos.*

17

2

2.1 Are you a student?

1 Vocabulary Countries and nationalities

A ▶2.1 Follow the instructions.
1. Do the country quiz. Match photos a–g to countries 1–7.
2. Read the text about nationalities. Then complete the words in the quiz.
3. Use the pink stressed letters to guess the pronunciation. Then listen, check, and repeat.

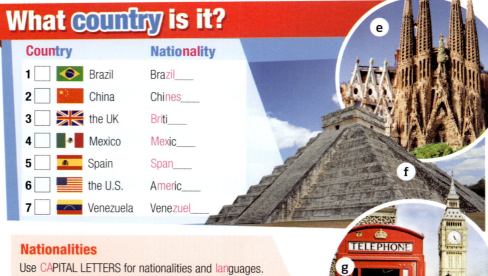

What **country** is it?

Country		Nationality
1 ☐ 🇧🇷 Brazil		Bra**zil**____
2 ☐ 🇨🇳 China		Chi**nes**____
3 ☐ 🇬🇧 the UK		**Bri**ti____
4 ☐ 🇲🇽 Mexico		**Mex**ic____
5 ☐ 🇪🇸 Spain		**Span**____
6 ☐ 🇺🇸 the U.S.		A**mer**ic____
7 ☐ 🇻🇪 Venezuela		Vene**zuel**____

Nationalities
Use CAPITAL LETTERS for nationalities and **lan**guages.
In the Americas, 35 nationalities end in *-an*, *-ian*, or *-ean*.
For ex**am**ple, Costa **Ric**an, Pe**ru**vian, **Chil**ean.
-ish and *-ese* are **com**mon **en**dings too.
For example, **Span**ish, Portu**guese**, Japa**nese**.

B ▶2.2 Listen and follow the model. Practice the sentences.

Where are you from? – Brazil.   I'm from Brazil. I'm Brazilian.

C 🅐 **Make it personal**   In pairs, ask and answer. Imagine new identities!

What's your name?   I'm Son Heung-min.

Where are you from?   I'm from Chuncheon. I'm South Korean.

2 Grammar *I am / you are* ➕ ➖

A ▶2.3 Read the *Guess who?* game. Who is it? Listen to check your answer.

Are you from Australia?
Yes, I am.
Ah, you're a woman. You aren't a man.
Correct.

Are you an actor?
No, I'm not.

OK, I'm a woman. I'm Australian. I'm not an actor. I'm a musician! Who am I?
I know! You're …

18

B Reread the game in **A** and complete the grammar box.

Positive ➕	Negative ➖
I _____ from Brazil.	I _____ a singer.
You _____ an actor.	You _____ a teacher.
Question ❓	**Short answers**
Am I a student?	Yes, I _____. / No, I _____.
_____ you Chilean?	Yes, you are. / No, you aren't.

➡ **Grammar 2A** p. 74

♪ And I got my hands up,
They're playing my song,
I know I'm gonna be ok,
Yeah, it's a party in the USA.

2.1

Common mistakes

~~P~~
Are you ~~p~~araguayan?

a
I'm ∧ politician.

C Circle the correct words.

1
A Your / You're Colombian.
B Correct!
A Am / Are you an actor?
B No, I'm not / I not.
A OK. You am not / aren't an actor. Am / Are you a musician?
B Yes, I am / I'm.
A Oh, you am / 're …!

2
A You're / Are you Puerto Rican?
B Yes, I am / am.
A Are / Are you a director?
B Yes, and I'm / I an actor too.
A Be / Are you …?

D 🗣 **Make it personal** In pairs, play **Guess who?**
A: Be a famous person. Draw or mime clues for your partner.
B: Ask questions and guess who **A** is. Then change roles.

Are you Latin American?

③ Vocabulary Numbers 13–20 and plurals

A ▶ 2.4 Match photos a–h to the numbers. Listen, check, and repeat.

☐ thir**teen**   ☐ fif**teen**   ☐ seven**teen**   ☐ nine**teen**
☐ four**teen**   ☐ six**teen**   ☐ eigh**teen**   ☐ twen**ty**

B ▶ 2.5 Listen and match the words to the photos in **A**. Then in pairs, cover the words and remember the phrase for each photo.

☐ a**part**ment   ☐ **chann**el   ☐ **doll**ars   ☐ **Ha**ppy **bir**thday
☐ **ki**los   ☐ **li**ters   ☐ miles per hour ☐ ki**lo**meters

Twenty dollars.

C 🗣 **Make it personal** In pairs, play the game, then change roles.
A: Write a number with your finger on **B**'s back.
B: Say the number.

2.2 Who's your favorite actor?

1 Grammar *he / she / it is* ⊕ ⊖ and personal pronouns

A Match headlines a–g to photos 1–7.

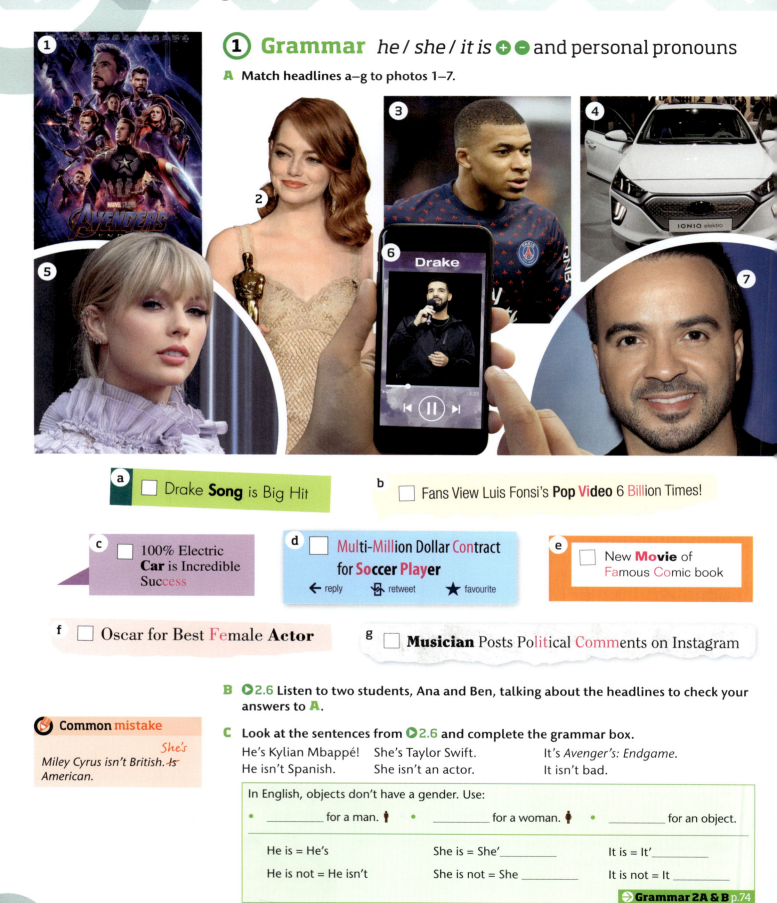

a ☐ Drake **Song** is Big Hit

b ☐ Fans View Luis Fonsi's **Pop Video** 6 **Bill**ion Times!

c ☐ 100% Electric **Car** is Incredible Su**cc**ess

d ☐ **Mu**lti-**Mill**ion Dollar **C**ontract for **So**ccer **Play**er
← reply　↻ retweet　★ favourite

e ☐ New **Movie** of **Fa**mous **C**omic book

f ☐ Oscar for Best **F**emale **Actor**

g ☐ **Musician** Posts Po**li**tical **C**omm**en**ts on Instagram

B ▶2.6 Listen to two students, Ana and Ben, talking about the headlines to check your answers to **A**.

⚠ Common mistake
　　　　　　　　She's
Miley Cyrus isn't British. ~~Is~~ American.

C Look at the sentences from ▶2.6 and complete the grammar box.

He's Kylian Mbappé!　　She's Taylor Swift.　　It's *Avenger's: Endgame*.
He isn't Spanish.　　　　She isn't an actor.　　 It isn't bad.

> In English, objects don't have a gender. Use:
> • _____ for a man. 🚹　• _____ for a woman. 🚺　• _____ for an object.
>
> He is = He's　　　　She is = She'_____　　It is = It'_____
> He is not = He isn't　She is not = She _____　It is not = It _____

➡ Grammar 2A & B p.74

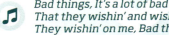

Bad things, It's a lot of bad things,
That they wishin' and wishin',
They wishin' on me, Bad things.

2.2

D In pairs, do the quiz. Circle the correct words. Then make sentences.

1. Hollywood is in **New York** / **Los Angeles**.
2. Penelope Cruz is **Spanish** / **Mexican**.
3. Justin Trudeau is **a Canadian** / **an American** politician.
4. A Porsche is **an Italian** / **a German** car.
5. Big Ben is in **Paris** / **London**.
6. Cardi B is **Brazilian** / **American**.
7. Sushi is **Japanese** / **Chinese**.
8. Shaun Mendes is **a director** / **a musician**.
9. Mohammed Salah is a **soccer player** / **dancer**.
10. Samsung is a **Chinese** / **South Korean** company.

Hollywood isn't in New York. It's in Los Angeles.

E ▶2.7 Listen and follow the model. Practice the sentences.

Taylor Swift is a musician.   *She's a musician.*   *A Porsche is a car.*   *It's a car.*

F 🔵 **Make it personal** In pairs, write six quiz sentences about famous people, places, and things. Give your quiz to another pair. How many do you get right?

② Vocabulary Adjectives (1)

A ▶2.8 Listen to Ana and Ben and check the four photos in **1A** they mention.

B ▶2.8 Listen again and circle the four adjectives from this chart that you hear. Then complete the speech bubbles. Remember to use *a* or *an*.

It's _____ song.

I think he's _____ musician.

I think she's _____ actor!

I think it's _____ movie!

C Study Common mistakes, then circle the correct rules in the grammar box.

Adjective order

Adjectives go **before** / **after** nouns and have **only one form** / **a singular and plural form**.

an American woman   two digital cameras   a fantastic car

➤ **Grammar 2C** p.74

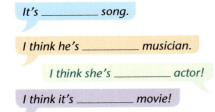

🔶 **Common mistakes**

She's an actor excellent.
I love restaurants Italian.
They're singers fantastic.

D Match sentences 1–4 to the responses.

1. Who's your favorite actor?
2. Ariana Grande is an incredible musician.
3. What's your favorite movie?
4. *Fortnite* is a terrible video game.

☐ I agree. She's fantastic!
☐ I disagree. I think it's good!
☐ Scarlett Johansson. I think she's incredible.
☐ *Bohemian Rhapsody*. I love the band Queen.

E ▶2.9 Listen and follow the model. Practice the sentences.

She's a very good politician. – Terrible.   *She's a terrible politician.*   *He*   *He's a terrible politician.*

F 🔵 **Make it personal** In groups, ask for and give opinions about your favorite people and things. Where possible, use the adjectives in **2B**. Any differences of opinion?

actor   animal   car   celebrity
city   fast food restaurant
pizza   musician   song   sport

What's your favorite fast food restaurant?

I don't know. / Hmm, it's a difficult question.

It's ... I think it's incredible.

Who's your favorite celebrity?

It's Bradley Cooper. He's fantastic.

I agree. / I disagree. I think he's ...

21

2.3 Is ceviche Mexican?

1 Grammar *Is he / she / it ...?*

A ▶ 2.10 Listen to Ana and Ben talking about *This Week* magazine. Which two photos do they talk about?

Images from around the world this week

B ▶ 2.10 Listen again, read, and complete the dialogue.

Ana Look at this __photo__.
Ben What's her name? Oh, I don't remember. She's a fantastic _____.
Ana Yes, and she's a model too! Is she from _____?
Ben No, she isn't! She's from _____. Oh, what's her _____?!
Ana Sorry, I don't remember. Hey, what's _____?
Ben It's a berimbau, a musical instrument.
Ana Wow! Is it _____?
Ben No, it isn't! It's from _____.
Ana What's the name again?
Ben A berimbau. Oh, and she's Sofía Vergara.
Ana Yes, correct!

C Reread the dialogue and complete the grammar box with *is* or *isn't*.

Question ?		Short answers				
____	he a student?	Yes,	he	____	No,	he	____
	she Mexican?		she			she	
	it a good pop video?		it			it	

➡ **Grammar 2A** p.74

D ▶ 2.11 Listen and follow the model. Practice the sentences.

She's Brazilian. Question.   *Is she Brazilian?*   *Negative.*   *She isn't Brazilian.*

E Put the words in order. Find the items in photos 1–7. Then write a similar dialogue for the other three photos.

1 A is / Who / he / ?
  B entrepreneur / He / an / 's
  A British / he / Is / ?
  B he / No, / isn't / 's / American / He

2 A this / 's / What / ?
  B game / It / video / 's / a
  A a / Is / game / it / good / ?
  B is / Yes, / it

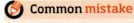
You are the dancing queen,
Young and sweet, only seventeen.

2.3

F 🗣 **Make it personal** In groups, play **10 questions**. Give your opinion of a very famous place / person / thing. Your group has only 10 chances to guess.

I think he's fantastic.   *No, he isn't.*   *Yes, he is.*
     OK, it's a man. Is he an actor?   *Is he American?*

⚠ **Common mistake**
What's ~~the name of he~~? *his*
Use *his* for a man, *her* for a woman.

② Vocabulary Numbers 20–100+ and plurals (2)

A ▶2.12 Match the words to the numbers. Listen, check, and write the extra word you hear for each number.

eighty   fifty   forty   a hundred   ninety
seventy   sixty   thirty   twenty

20 _____   30 _____   40 _____   50 _____   60 _____

70 _____   80 _____   90 _____   100 _____

B ▶2.13 Listen and ⓒircle the correct ages.

1 21 / 22 / 23   2 36 / 38 / 41   3 49 / 54 / 62   4 75 / 85 / 95

C ▶2.14 Listen and follow the model. Practice the numbers.

12 + 3   *fifteen*   24 + 10   *thirty-four*

D 🗣 **Make it personal** Read the information and answer 1–4.

Numbers
- Use a hyphen in numbers from 21 to 99: *twenty-one, thirty-two, forty-three.*
- Say years as two numbers: 1998 = *nineteen ninety-eight*; 2018 = *twenty eighteen.*
- To talk about age, use *be* + age + *years old* (optional): *I'm seventeen (years old).*

1 What year is it? And the next three years?
2 What's your year of birth?
3 What's your lucky number?
4 How old are you? Ask the whole class and form an age line.

⚠ **Common mistakes**
How ~~many years you have~~? *old are you?*
I ~~have~~ 19 ~~years~~! *am* *old*

How old are you?
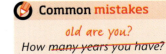
I'm … years and … months old.

2.4 Where are your two favorite places?

1 Vocabulary Adjectives (2)

A ▶2.15 Match photos 1–14 to these adjectives. Listen, check, and repeat.

beautiful ☐ / ugly ☐   hot ☐ / cold ☐   big ☐ / small ☐
expensive ☐ / cheap ☐   friendly ☐ / unfriendly ☐
old ☐ / new ☐   happy ☐ / unhappy ☐

B ▶2.16 Listen and follow the model. Practice the opposite adjectives.

> What's the opposite of hot?

> cold

C **Make it personal** In pairs, write a sentence (true or false) for each adjective. Exchange your sentences with another pair and guess true or false.

> The students in this school are friendly.
> My tablet is very old!

> It's true. The students are very friendly.

2 Reading

A ▶2.17 Read and listen to the online chat and circle the correct answers.
1. Roberto and Maria are on vacation in **Bogotá** / **Lima** / **Mexico City**.
2. They are having **a terrible** / **a great** time.

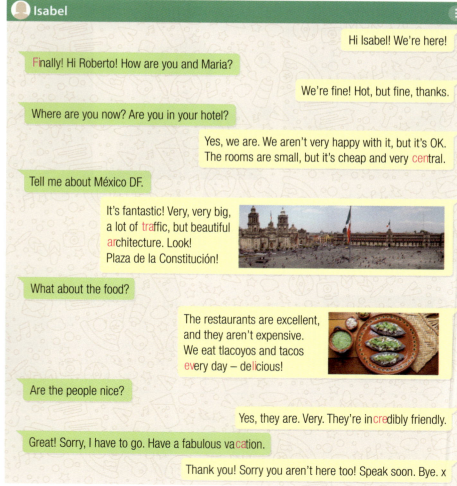

Isabel

> Hi Isabel! We're here!

> Finally! Hi Roberto! How are you and Maria?

> We're fine! Hot, but fine, thanks.

> Where are you now? Are you in your hotel?

> Yes, we are. We aren't very happy with it, but it's OK. The rooms are small, but it's cheap and very central.

> Tell me about México DF.

> It's fantastic! Very, very big, a lot of traffic, but beautiful architecture. Look! Plaza de la Constitución!

> What about the food?

> The restaurants are excellent, and they aren't expensive. We eat tlacoyos and tacos every day – delicious!

> Are the people nice?

> Yes, they are. Very. They're incredibly friendly.

> Great! Sorry, I have to go. Have a fabulous vacation.

> Thank you! Sorry you aren't here too! Speak soon. Bye. x

B Test your memory. Cover the online chat in **2A**. Which adjectives in **1A** describe …
   1 the hotel?
   2 the city?
   3 the food?
   4 the people?

🎵 *Are we human, or are we dancer? My sign is vital, my hands are cold, And I'm on my knees looking for the answer.* **2.4**

3 Grammar *you / we / they are* ➕ ➖ ❓

A Reread the chat in **2A** and complete the plural forms in the grammar box.

Positive ➕	Negative ➖
You're fine.	You _____ unhappy.
We _____ finally here.	We _____ in an expensive hotel.
They _____ very friendly.	They _____ difficult.

Question ❓		Short answers					
_____	you in your hotel?	Yes,	we		No,	we	
	we good friends?		you	_____		you	aren't.
	the restaurants expensive?		they			they	

Contractions: _____ = you are   we're = we are   _____ = they are

Common mistakes

Are the tacos
~~The tacos are~~ delicious?
  they are. Very.
Yes, ~~are very.~~

➡ Grammar 2A p.74

B ▶ 2.18 Listen and follow the model. Practice the sentences.

They're friendly. – Negative.   They aren't friendly.   Question.   Are they friendly?

C ▶ 2.19 Read the message and add *is / isn't* and *are / aren't*. Use contractions where possible. Listen to check.

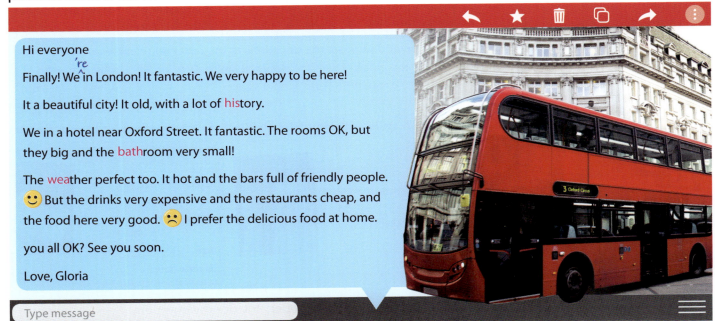

Hi everyone
Finally! We ˄'re in London! It   fantastic. We   very happy to be here!

It   a beautiful city! It   old, with a lot of history.

We   in a hotel near Oxford Street. It   fantastic. The rooms   OK, but they   big and the bathroom   very small!

The weather   perfect too. It   hot and the bars   full of friendly people. 🙂 But the drinks   very expensive and the restaurants   cheap, and the food here   very good. ☹ I prefer the delicious food at home.

   you all OK? See you soon.

Love, Gloria

D 🗣 **Make it personal** *Fantasy vacation!* In pairs, imagine you're on a special vacation. Imagine the place, the hotel, the food, the people, what's good and what's bad. Write an online chat with a friend at home.

	Lucas	Hi! How are you? We're in Paris now.
	Emilia	Is the hotel nice?
	Lucas	Yes, it's fantastic! The rooms are beautiful, but they're expensive.

2.5 Is English essential for your future?

Skills Reading for general comprehension

A Read the text. Choose the best ending for the title. Which other languages are international?

1 essential for Latin America   2 a global language   3 the language of business

English – ...

English is an essential language in the modern world. In over 100 countries, it is part of the school curriculum and the most important international language for government, education, business, media, and art. Chinese politicians use English to communicate with American politicians, Brazilian artists with Nigerian artists, Russian scientists with Japanese scientists. Globally, over two billion people speak or study English.

It's THE international language of this planet.

B ▶2.20 Listen and reread. Underline all the cognates. Then circle the words you don't understand. In pairs, can you guess the meaning?

Common mistake

I need ~~the~~ English for ~~the~~ job. *(my)*

C Why do you need English? Check your top three reasons. Can you find a classmate with exactly the same reasons?

- [ ] to travel
- [ ] to meet and communicate with new people
- [ ] to get a good job
- [ ] to study in the future
- [ ] to get a certificate
- [ ] to understand music and movies
- [ ] for pleasure

D ▶2.21 Listen and number the questions in the order you hear them, 1–9.

- [ ] Who are the girls?
- [ ] Where are they from?
- [ ] Where's he from?
- [ ] How old are they?
- [ ] Who's she?
- [ ] How old is he?
- [ ] Is he married?
- [ ] Where's she from?
- [ ] What city is he from?

E ▶2.21 Listen again and complete profiles 1–3. Are they famous in your country?

1
Name: Ryan Gosling / actor
Nationality: _____ (London, Ontario)
Age: _____
Marital status: _____

2
Name: Girls Generation / musicians
Nationality: _____ (Seoul)
Age: _____
Marital status: _____

3
Name: Simona Halep / tennis player
Nationality: _____ (Constanta)
Age: _____
Marital status: _____

F ▶2.22 Listen and follow the model. Practice the questions.

How old – she   How old is she?

G 🗣 **Make it personal** In pairs, ask questions and complete the form. Change partners, and ask and answer about your old partners.

What city are you from?

Where's your old partner from?

Name: _____   City: _____
Nationality: _____   Marital status: _____
Age: _____

How old is Ariana Grande?

♪ We're up all night to the sun.
We're up all night to get some.
We're up all night for good fun.
We're up all night to get lucky.

2.5

ID in Action Sharing information about other people

A ▶ 2.23 Match 1–6 to the responses. Listen, check, and repeat.

1 Where's he from?
2 Are you sure?
3 How old is he?
4 Is he married?
5 How old are they?
6 She's a tennis player.

☐ You're right. Number one in the world.
☐ I don't know. No idea.
☐ Yes, he is.
☐ 1 I think he's from the U.S.
☐ Hmm. No, he's Canadian!
☐ He's around 38.

B Respond to 1–6. Use the expressions in **A** to help you. In pairs, practice.

1 Justin Bieber is a fantastic singer.
2 Ariana Grande is British.
3 How old is Adam Levine?
4 Is Adele married?
5 Coldplay are American tennis players.
6 Are Kim Kardashian and Kanye West married?

C 🗣 **Make it personal** In groups, share information about these celebrities. Do you know them all?

the JB · Married? · DL · From? · Who? · VD · LS · ND · BE · MM & CA · ZE · Your opinion? · How old?

Who's Dua Lipa? I have no idea. I think she's an American singer. No, she's from the UK.

27

Writing 2   A blog post

*Maybe I'm crazy,
Maybe you're crazy,
Maybe we're crazy,
Probably ooh hmm.*

A ▶ 2.24 Look at the photos on Victor's blog post. Where is he? Read the first sentence and check.

B Read the blog post and put sentences 1–4 in the correct place.
1. It's small, but the breakfast in the morning is very big!
2. Where are you at the moment?
3. Mission Dolores was founded in 1776.
4. It's not very hot, but not too cold.

Home   Blog   About   Contact

Victor's Adventures

It's fantastic here in San Francisco, California! We're very happy. It's a beautiful city with a lot of history. Parts of the city are very old. ☐ And the cable cars are from 1873! We're in a new hotel near Lombard Street. ☐ That's good because restaurants are expensive here. The people are very friendly in this city, and the weather is perfect. ☐ What about you? ☐ Tell me in the comments below.

C Read *Write it right!* Find the 11 adjectives Victor uses to describe 1–7.
1. the city (2) *fantastic* _____
2. parts of San Francisco (1) _____
3. the people (1) _____
4. the weather (3) _____ _____ _____
5. the restaurants (1) _____
6. the hotel (2) _____ _____
7. the breakfast (1) _____

✓ **Write it right!**

Use a variety of adjectives to make your writing interesting. Adjectives do NOT have plural forms.
The hotels are cheap. NOT ~~cheaps~~
Use a plural verb after *people*.
The people are very nice. NOT ~~The people is …~~

D Singular or plural? Circle the correct form of *be*.
1. The food here in Peru **is** / **are** delicious.
2. My city **is** / **are** famous for chocolate cakes.
3. The famous places there **isn't** / **aren't** very interesting.
4. Costa Rican bananas **is** / **are** incredible, and cheap.
5. The taxis in Switzerland **is** / **are** very, very expensive.
6. The big hotel in my street **isn't** / **aren't** very good.

E Think of a place you know or want to visit. Write one or two different adjectives to describe the following:
- the city
- parts of the city
- the people
- the weather
- the food
- the restaurants
- other famous or important things

F 🎧 **Make it personal**   Imagine you are visiting your place from **E**. Write a blog post about it.

Before	Read Victor's blog and plan what you want to say.
While	Use your adjectives in **E** to describe your place. Check the forms of the verb *be*.
After	Share your blog post with a partner. Check it for mistakes. Send it to your teacher.

2 People, places, passports!

 Café

1 Before watching

A Look at the flags and characters. Then, in pairs, ask and answer about their nationalities.

Where's she from? What's her nationality?

She's from Argentina and the U.S. She's Argentinian and American.

2 While watching

A Watch until 0:57. Circle the correct word.
1 Daniel's friend is a computer **programmer** / **technician**.
2 The computer server is **up** / **down**.
3 Their yoga class is on **Monday** / **Tuesday**.
4 Lucy, August and Andrea go to the **Argentinian** / **International** school.
5 Lucy's **American** / **Argentinian** now.
6 Daniel's from the **Midwest** / **South**.

B Watch from 0:57 to 1:36 and check Daniel (D), Rory (R), Lucy (L), or Genevieve (G). Where's Andrea now?

D	R	L	G	
				goes to computer class.
				is American.
				is Canadian.
				is originally Irish.
				has a new passport.
				is from two countries.

C Watch from 1:36 to the end. Who's ...
1 Lucy's favourite actor?
2 almost 19?
3 20 in July?
4 giving a party on Friday?
5 invited to the party?
6 going to a class now?

D Watch the last part and write the girls' phone numbers.

3 After watching

A Order the words in 1–5 to make questions. In pairs, ask and answer. Use contractions.
1 you / where / from / are / originally / ?
2 birthday / your / when / 's / ?
3 your / cell / what / 's / number / ?
4 favorite / who / 's / your / actor / ?
5 he / from / she / or / where / 's / ?

Where are you from originally from?

I'm from Montevideo, Uruguay.

B What do we say? Check the situation for expressions 1–10: introductions (I), asking for information (AFI) or giving personal information (GPI).

Expressions	I	AFI	GPI
1 You're the computer technician here, right?			
2 You're from that yoga class, right?			
3 Lucy, meet Rory.			
4 I'm originally from Dublin, Ireland.			
5 Daniel, this is Genevieve.			
6 Good to meet you.			
7 My birthday's in July.			
8 Nice meeting you too.			
9 Oh. It's 847-555-1976.			
10 I'm almost 17.			

C **Make it personal** In pairs, ask and answer using expressions from **B**.

Are you almost 21?

No, I'm only 18!

I'm sorry. When's your birthday?

It's October 4th.

R1 Grammar and vocabulary

A *Picture dictionary.* Cover the words on these pages and remember.

page	
7	numbers 1–12
	12 items similar in your language
8	6 classroom language expressions
10	12 classroom objects
12	26 letters of the alphabet
14	pronunciation of 11 cognates
15	5 ways to say *Hi*, and 5 ways to say *Bye*
18	7 countries and nationalities
19	numbers 13–20 and 7 plural nouns
21	8 opinion adjectives
23	numbers 20–100
24	14 more opinion adjectives

B *Make it personal* Choose a verb and write a list of instructions with that verb. Compare your lists—score 1 point for each correct sentence. Who's the winner?

listen (to)   look (at)   read   repeat
say   write

Say your name.
Don't say...
_____
_____

C Add the verb *be* in the correct place. Use contractions where possible.
1 What your name?
2 How old you?
3 you married?
4 What your phone number?
5 Who Greta Thunberg?
6 Robert Pattinson from the UK?
7 Where the Backstreet Boys from?
8 this a pen or a pencil?

D ▶R1.1 Now complete the answers and match them to questions 1–8 in **C**. Listen to check.
☐ Yes, he _____. He's from London.
☐ Yes, I _____. But I don't have children.
☐ She _____ a young activist from Sweden.
☐ It _____ a mechanical pencil!
☐ They _____ from Orlando. _____ American.
☐ I _____ 23 years old. And you?
☐ My name _____ Carmen.
☐ My cell? It _____ 41-8777-4883.

E *Make it personal* In pairs, ask and answer 1–4 in **C** and adapt 5–8 with locally relevant examples.

F Work in pairs. A: Spell the name of a country. B: Say what the nationality is. Then change roles.

A country: C-H-I-N-A. The nationality?   Chinese.

G Write four addition problems. Don't show them to your partner. Say them for your partner to answer.

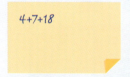

4+7+18   What's four plus seven plus eighteen?
   Twenty-nine.

H In groups of three, play *Mime!* Choose three items from photos in units 1 and 2. Mime them for your partners to name. Then change roles.

What's this?   I think it's a tablet.

I Correct the mistakes. Check your answers in units 1 and 2.

Common mistakes
1 Please look the text and listen the dialogue. (2 mistakes)
2 I from Brazil. Where you from? (2 mistakes)
3 Hello, good night! Good meet you! (2 mistakes)
4 Mariah Carey's musician. (1 mistake)
5 Who's she? Is British actor. (2 mistakes)
6 This's car. (2 mistakes)
7 What's this? Is my new tablet. (1 mistake)
8 You are a doctor? (1 mistake)
9 She's singer fantastic! (2 mistakes)
10 I have 35 years. (2 mistakes)

Skills practice

♪ *I am a giant. Stand up on my shoulders, tell me what you see.*
I am a giant. (We'll be breaking boulders underneath our feet.)

R1

A ▶R1.2 Read the website bio and guess the missing words 1–12. Listen to check.

First name: Camila Carraro
Last [1]_____ : Mendes
Date of birth: June 29, 1994

Camila Mendes is [2]_____ American actor. She's [3]_____ Virginia, USA, but her family [4]_____ from Brazil. Camila is a [5]_____ beautiful woman, [6]_____ she's [7]_____ a number of movies. But she's internationally [8]_____ for her part in the teen drama series *Riverdale* as Veronica Lodge. In the series, Veronica [9]_____ the daughter of Hiram Lodge, the richest [10]_____ in Riverdale. Camila [11]_____ also a graduate of the New York University Tisch School of the Arts. She speaks English and fluent [12]_____.

B Reread and answer.
1. How old is Camila Mendes now?
2. True (T) or false (F)?
   a. Camila's Brazilian.
   b. She's a movie and television actor.
   c. She's famous in many countries.
   d. Her father is Hiram Lodge.

C 🎧 **Make it personal** Write your opinion of 1–4. Use adjectives from p. 18. Compare opinions with a partner. Do you agree?

actor   car   movie   musician

1. The BMW: *I think it's a fantastic car.*
2. Miley Cyrus: _____
3. Maggie Gylennhaal: _____
4. *Avengers: Endgame*: _____

D Choose a celebrity or place from the photos in unit 2 or your imagination. Work in pairs. **A:** Give information for **B** to guess who she, he, or it is. Then change roles.

She's an excellent American actor. She's about 30 years old, and I don't think she's married.

Is she Emma Stone?

E ▶R1.3 Listen. Where's Alessandra from?

F ▶R1.3 Complete the dialogue with these words. Listen to check. Practice in groups of three.

agree	are	call	city	evening	from
Italian	meet	nice	right	see
thanks	this	too	where	you

Eddy Good _____, Paul. Good to _____ you.
Paul Hello, Eddy. How are _____?
Eddy I'm fine, _____. Paul, _____ is my friend Alessandra.
Paul Nice to _____ you, Alessandra.
Sandra _____ to meet you _____. Please, _____ me Sandra.
Paul _____ are you from, Sandra? Italy?
Eddy Yes, you're _____. She's _____.
Paul _____ you from Rome?
Sandra No, I'm _____ Siena.
Paul Wow! Siena's a beautiful _____!
Sandra Yes, I _____!

G Mini role-play.
A: You and **B** are friends. Say hello. But you don't know **C**.
B: You're friends with **A** and **C**. Introduce **A** to **C**.
C: You don't know **A**. Respond to the introduction. Look at the dialogue in **F** for help.

H ▶R1.4 Listen to an interview with a student and complete column A in the form.

	A	B
Name		
Nationality		
Marital status	☐ single ☐ married ☐ divorced ☐ other	☐ single ☐ married ☐ divorced ☐ other
Age		
Phone number		
Email		

I 🎧 **Make it personal** In pairs, interview your partner and complete column B in the form.

J 🎧 **Make it personal** *Question time.*
In pairs, practice asking and answering the 12 lesson titles in units 1 and 2. Use the book map on p. 2–3. Where possible, ask follow-up questions, too. Can you comfortably ask and answer all the questions?

What's your name?

My name's / I'm Ricardo, but call me Rick.

3

3.1 What do you do?

1 Vocabulary Jobs

A ▶3.1 How do you pronounce jobs a–e? Listen to an ad for a TV show to check. Then match photos 1–5 to jobs f–j.

a ___ bank ca**sh**ier
b ___ **doc**tor
c ___ engin**eer**
d ___ po**lice o**fficer
e ___ uni**ver**sity pro**fes**sor

☐ f ___ **law**yer /lɔjər/
☐ g ___ **ser**ver
☐ h ___ **hair**dresser
☐ i ___ **sales** clerk /seɪlsklɜrk/
☐ j ___ IT pro**fes**sional

B Read the information and Common mistakes, then complete the jobs in **A** with *a* or *an*.

> The usual question for jobs is:
> *What do you do? What does he / she do?*
> To answer, use verb *be* + *a* / *an*:
> *I'm a student. / He's a den**tist**.*
> Be careful with adjectives: *He's re**tired**.*

Common mistakes

What ~~/~~ you do? → do
I'm ~~/~~ doctor and she's ~~/~~ architect. → a, an
I'm ~~an~~ unemployed.
They're ~~a~~ doctors.

C ▶3.2 Listen to the TV show and match eight jobs from **A** to the participants. Which two jobs are not mentioned?

32

D ◉3.3 Listen to extracts 1–9 and say *He / She* and the correct job in **A** after the beep.

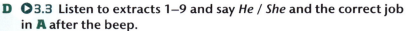
♪ *I want to be the one to walk in the sun,*
Oh girls they want to have fun,
Oh girls just want to have fun.

3.1

E In pairs, try to remember the people's jobs in **C**.

Tessa's a hairdresser.

F 🙂 **Make it personal**

1 What do you do or what do you want to do? Ask your teacher for the name of your job in English if necessary. Complete the sentences.

| I'm _____. | I want to be _____. |

2 Ask your classmates about their jobs. Are you a student? What do you want to be? How many different jobs are there in the class?

What do you do?   *What do you want to be?*

I'm unemployed.   *I want to be a lawyer.*

② Listening and Vocabulary Job suffixes

A ◉3.4 Listen to part two of *Fantastic Families*. Check the characters you hear and match them to their jobs.

Amy Farrah Fowler
The Big Bang Theory ☐

Ross Geller
Friends ☐

Jessica Pearson
Suits ☐

Conrad Hawkins
The Resident ☐

☐ doctor   ☐ lawyer   ☐ scientist   ☐ university professor

B ◉3.5 Listen and follow the model. Practice the sentences.

Ross Geller – university professor   *He's a university professor.*

C Look at the characters and jobs in **A** again. What do the others do? Guess if you don't know.

I think Amy Farrah Fowler is a …   *You're right. / I'm not sure. / I don't know. / You're wrong.*

D ◉3.6 The most common suffixes for jobs are *-er* and *-or*. Complete these jobs, then use an online dictionary to check. Listen to the pronunciation.

an act___   a manag___   a profess___   a teach___
a bank___   a movie direct___   a programm___   a writ___
a doct___   an office work___   a serv___
a hairdress___ a paint___   a soccer play___
a lawy___   a police offic___   a taxi driv___

E 🙂 **Make it personal** In groups, mime a job for the others to guess.   *You're a writer.*

33

3.2 Do you have brothers and sisters?

The next king

The royal family is the most famous family in the UK. Queen Elizabeth and her husband Philip are very old, and their son Charles is next in line to be king, and after him, his first son William. (William's brother Harry is not in line.) William has three children: two sons (George and Louis) and a daughter (Charlotte). Kate is their mother. George is third in line to be king after his father and his grandfather.

1 Reading

Common mistakes

My family is big. I have a lot of ~~parents~~.
   relatives
      parents
My ~~fathers~~ live in Madrid.
   siblings
I have two ~~brothers~~: Lucy and Jack.

A ▶3.7 Listen to and read the text about the British royal family. Who are the next kings? Order the names, 1–3. One name is not used.

☐ Charles ☐ George ☐ Harry ☐ William

2 Vocabulary Family and possessive adjectives

A ▶3.8 Reread the text in **1A** and complete the table with the highlighted words. Listen, check, and repeat.

Female	Male	Both
mother		parents
wife		couple
	son	
sister		siblings
grandmother		grandparents

B Find George in the photo in **1A** then complete his family tree.

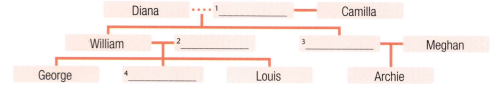

C In groups of three, follow the instructions. Then change roles.

A: Say a female form.   B: Say the male form.   C: Say the word for both.

34

D Read *Mystery Man* and guess who he is. Notice the bold words, then circle the correct word in 1–3.
1 My husband is a doctor. **His** / **Your** name's Bruce.
2 This is my sister. **Our** / **Her** name's Teresa.
3 These are my parents. **They** / **Their** names are Joy and Felix.

Whether you're a brother or whether you're a mother, You're stayin' alive, stayin' alive.

→ Grammar 3A p.76

MYSTERY MAN

Our mystery man today is from Rosario, Argentina. He's married. **His** wife is a model. **Her** name is Antonella. They have three sons. **Their** names are Thiago, Mateo, and Ciro. He has tattoos of all **his** children. In my opinion, he's the best soccer player of **his** generation.

E **Make it personal** Play *Mystery person*. Write a text about a famous person (dead or alive). Go online for information if necessary. In pairs, take turns reading your text. Can your partner guess who it is?

I'm from Mexico and I'm an artist. My husband's Mexican. His name's Diego. He's an artist, too.

Are you Frida Kahlo?

3 Grammar Simple present: *I / you / we / they* ⊕ ⊖ ❓

A ▶ 3.9 Listen and match conversations 1–3 to pictures a–c.

Common mistakes

Her
~~She~~ name's Jessica.

                 to
Meghan is married ~~with~~ Harry.

Their
~~His~~ last name is Windsor.

B ▶ 3.10 Complete extracts 1–3 with these words. Listen, check, and repeat.

don't   family   ~~have~~   live   son   with

1 **A** Do you ___have___ children?
  B Yes, I do. I have a _____.

2 **A** Do you _____ alone?
  B No, I don't. I live _____ my grandmother.

3 **A** Do you have a big _____?
  B No, I _____ have siblings. I'm an only child.

C Complete the grammar box with *do* or *don't*. Notice *don't* = *do not*.

Positive ⊕	Negative ⊖	Questions ❓	Short answers
I have two brothers. I live with my parents.	I don't have a big family. I _____ live alone.	Do you have siblings? _____ you live alone?	Yes, I _____. No, I _____.

→ Grammar 3B p.76

D ▶ 3.11 Listen and follow the model. Practice the questions and answers.

children – question   *Do you have children?*   children – negative   *I don't have children.*

E Match 1–6 to the responses. Who is the "mystery woman"?

1 Do you have brothers and sisters?
2 What is his name?
3 Do you have children?
4 Do you live alone?
5 Are you married?
6 What's your husband's name?

☐ His name's Barack.
☐ Yes, I am.
☐ Yes, I do. I have a brother.
☐ Yes, I have two daughters. Their names are Malia and Sasha.
☐ My brother's name is Craig.
☐ No, I don't. I live with my family.

Common mistakes

Do you
~~You~~ live alone?

don't
I ~~not~~ have a car.

F **Make it personal** In pairs, ask and answer questions like those in **E**. Who has more brothers or sisters? Who lives with the most people? Who has the most animals?

3.3 Do you have a job?

1 Vocabulary Places of work

A Guess the pronunciation of the places in group 1. Then match photos a–e to the places in group 2. In pairs, check your answers.

> **Common mistakes**
>
> ~~Where you work?~~ *do*
> ~~I work in the downtown.~~
> ~~I work in the factory.~~ *a*
> ~~I work in home.~~ *at*
> ~~She's not here. She's in school.~~ *at*

1.
- in a bank ___
- in a hospital ___
- in a restaurant ___
- in a school __1__

2.
- ☐ downtown ___
- ☐ in a drugstore ___
- ☐ at home ___
- ☐ in an office ___
- ☐ in a travel agency ___

B ▶3.12 Listen to the start of a podcast and number the places in **A** in the order you hear them, 1–9. What's the podcast about?

C Cover the words in **A**. In pairs, remember the nine places.

2 Listening

A ▶3.13 Listen to the podcast and complete the sentences with their second job. Check their favorite job.

PEOPLE WITH TWO JOBS
- Who are they?
- What do they do?
- Where do they work?

▶ Listen to this week's podcast and meet Hanna and Victor.

Hanna Randal is a personal assistant ☐ and a _____ ☐.

Victor Bell is a freelance web designer ☐ and a _____ ☐.

B ▶3.13 Listen again. Where do they work? Write Hanna (H) or Victor (V) next to the four places in **1A**.

C ▶3.14 Listen to and repeat the four sentences. Connect the *k* in *work* to the prepositions.

> I work in a drugstore.

3 Grammar Simple present

Do you really want to hurt me?
Do you really want to make me cry?

A ▶3.15 Complete 1–6 in the grammar box. Listen to check.

Yes / No questions A S I

Auxiliary	Subject	Infinitive
1 _____	you	work at home?
2 _____	you	want to be a doctor?
3 _____	you	live here?

Wh- questions Q A S I

Question word	Auxiliary	Subject	Infinitive
4 _____	_do_	you	do?
5 Where	_____	you	work?
6 Where	_____	you	want to work?

→ **Grammar 3B** p. 76

B Match these answers to questions 1–6 in **A**. In pairs, practice asking and answering.
- ☐ No, I don't. I want to be a lawyer. It's an interesting job.
- ☐ I'm a bank cashier. I like it very much.
- ☐ I want to work at home. No traffic!
- ☐ Yes, apartment 61. It's a beautiful apartment.
- ☐ Yes, I do. I work freelance. It's great.
- ☐ I work in an office in Ventura.

C ▶3.16 Listen and follow the model. Practice the questions and answers. Copy the sentence stress.

work – question   **Where** do you **work**?   an office   I **work** in an **office**.

D 🔊 Make it personal **Work, work, work!**
1. Do the questionnaire. Answer question 1. Then put a ✓ or ✗ in the first box for each place in question 2.
2. In pairs, ask and answer. Complete the second box with your partner's answers.
3. Do you and your partner have anything in common?
4. What are the most popular answers in your class? What are the least popular?

DO YOU KNOW WHAT'S BEST FOR YOU?

1. What do you (want to) do?   I'm (I want to be) _____ .
2. Do you (want to) work:
   - at home? ☐ ☐
   - in an office? ☐ ☐
   - in a store? ☐ ☐
   - in a bank? ☐ ☐
   - downtown? ☐ ☐
   - freelance? ☐ ☐
   - online? ☐ ☐
   - in a **fac**tory? ☐ ☐

We (want to) work in an office.
I (want to) work in a bank.

We don't (want to) work freelance.

3.4 Where does your mother work?

PEOPLE WITH UNUSUAL JOBS
This week we interview Natesh, a New York City limo driver.

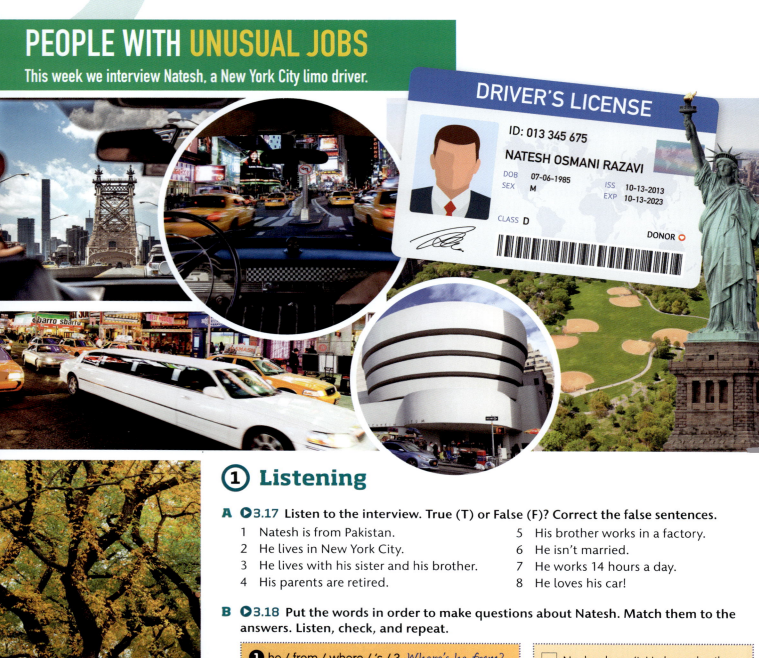

1 Listening

A ▶3.17 Listen to the interview. True (T) or False (F)? Correct the false sentences.
1. Natesh is from Pakistan.
2. He lives in New York City.
3. He lives with his sister and his brother.
4. His parents are retired.
5. His brother works in a factory.
6. He isn't married.
7. He works 14 hours a day.
8. He loves his car!

B ▶3.18 Put the words in order to make questions about Natesh. Match them to the answers. Listen, check, and repeat.

1. he / from / where / 's / ? *Where's he from?*
2. does / he / where / live / ?
3. alone / live / he / does / ?
4. a sister / does / have / he / ?
5. he / is / married / ?
6. what / do / he / does / ?
7. he / work / where / does / ?
8. his / he / does / job / like / ?

- [ ] No, he doesn't. He has a brother.
- [ ] He's a limo driver.
- [ ] Yes, he does. Very much.
- [1] He's from Pakistan.
- [ ] No, but he has a girlfriend.
- [ ] No, he lives with his family.
- [ ] He works in Manhattan.
- [ ] He lives in New York City.

C 🎤 **Make it personal** Cover the answers in **B**. In pairs, ask and answer the questions to test your partner's memory. Do you like to drive? Do you know anyone with an unusual job?

Yes, I do. My cousin, Nico. He's a bed tester.

My brother works part-time at night in a grocery store.

2 Grammar Simple present: he / she / it ➕ ➖ ❓

🎵 Oh, whatever it takes,
'Cause I love the adrenaline in my veins,
I do whatever it takes,
'Cause I love how it feels when I break the chains.

3.4

A Look at the sentences and questions in **1A** and **1B** and study Common mistakes. Complete the grammar box with these verbs.

does (x2)   doesn't (x3)   has   have   like   live (x2)   lives   work   works

Positive ➕ – verb + s		Negative ➖ SAI	
He She	_____ a brother. _____ in an office. _____ in an apartment.	He She	_____ a sister. _____ on weekends. _____ alone.
Questions ❓ ASI, QASI		**Short answers Yes / No + SIA**	
Does	he she	_____ his job? work downtown? _____ with a friend?	Yes, he she _____ . No, he she _____ .
What Where Where	_____	he she	do? he work? she live?	Contractions: _____ = does not

Common mistakes
has
Suri ~~have~~ a daughter.
work
She doesn't ~~works~~ at home.
doesn't
She ~~don't~~ live with her mother.

→ Grammar 3C p. 76

B ▶ 3.19 Listen and follow the model. Practice the sentences.

I live alone. – He   He lives alone.   I have a brother. – She   She has a brother.

C Read and complete the text with these verbs.

drives   have   live   lives

> Apart from the verb *be*, English verbs have only two simple present forms.
> *I, you, we, they* + verb.
> We _____ here. I _____ a bike.
> *He, she, it* + verb + *s*.
> He _____ there. She _____ a car.
> Make your teacher happy! Don't forget the **s**!

D 🔵 **Make it personal**

1 Complete the 🆔 form for a member of your family.

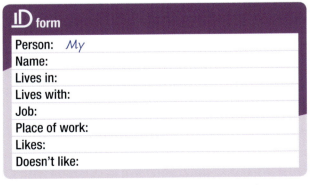

🆔 form	
Person:	My
Name:	
Lives in:	
Lives with:	
Job:	
Place of work:	
Likes:	
Doesn't like:	

2 In pairs, ask and answer to get information about your partner's person. Show a photo if you can.

Who's this person?   What does she do?   Does she work in a restaurant?

She's my mother.   She's a chef.   No, she works in a hotel.

3.5 Do you live near here?

Skills Listening for specific information

A ▶3.20 Listen to and read the information. Then look at the photo of Laura and Charlie and try to predict the answers to questions 1–3.

Maybe they're friends on vacation.

> **Listening for specific information**
> Listening isn't easy — in any language!
> Here are three listening tips:
> 1 Before you listen, imagine the context, and the words or phrases people use in that situation.
> 2 Know your objective: What exactly do I need to understand?
> 3 Don't expect to understand or mentally translate every word. It isn't necessary.

1 What four questions do they ask?
  a Do you like this music?
  b Do you like this food?
  c Do you like this class?
  d Do you live near here?
  e How are you?
  f Is that good?
  g What about you?
  h What do you do?
  i What do you study?
  j What do you want to eat?

2 Where are they?
  a at a party
  b at work
  c at school

3 What is their relationship?
  a brother and sister
  b husband and wife
  c just friends
  d strangers

B ▶3.21 Listen to part one of their conversation to check.

C ▶3.21 Check the 10 words Laura and Charlie use. Listen again to check.

☐ beautiful	☐ hi	☐ music	☐ teacher
☐ computer	☐ incredible	☐ nice	☐ unemployed
☐ fantastic	☐ interesting	☐ office	☐ university
☐ hello	☐ live	☐ student	☐ work

D ▶3.22 Listen to the complete conversation and write Charlie (C) or Laura (L) in 1–9.
1 ___ lives downtown.
2 ___ lives near here.
3 ___ is unemployed.
4 ___ studies IT.
5 ___ is an IT professional.
6 ___ works for a bank.
7 ___ isn't married.
8 ___ doesn't live alone.
9 ___ ends the conversation.

E ▶3.22 Listen again. How much can you understand: 50% / 60% / 80% / 100%? Go to AS 3.22 on p. 86 to check. In pairs, read the dialogue out loud. Change some of the information.

What do you do? — *I'm a nurse.*

F 🅐 **Make it personal** In pairs. What do / don't you have in common with Charlie and Laura?

Charlie lives with his partner, and I live with my partner.

Laura is unemployed. I'm not unemployed. I have a job.

Where do you study?

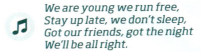

*We are young we run free,
Stay up late, we don't sleep,
Got our friends, got the night
We'll be all right.*

3.5

ID in Action Exchanging personal information

A ▶3.23 Match questions 1–10 to the answers. Listen, check, and repeat. In pairs, ask the questions and give your own answers.

10 QUESTIONS TO ASK AT A PARTY

1. Do you live near here?
2. Do you live alone?
3. Do you have brothers and sisters?
4. Do you have children?
5. Do you have a boyfriend?
6. What do you do?
7. Where do you study?
8. Where does your father work?
9. What does your wife do?
10. How old are your children?

- [ ] Yes, I do. Two daughters.
- [ ] I'm an engineer.
- [ ] No, I live with my parents.
- [ ] He's retired.
- [ ] She's a university professor.
- [ ] Yes, I have one brother.
- [ ] No, I live downtown.
- [ ] Yes, I do. His name's Simon.
- [ ] They're 7 and 10.
- [ ] At UCLA.

B Imagine you're at a party. Think of six other questions to ask a person you don't know.

> What do you study?   Where do you work?

C ▶3.24 In conversation, be positive to show you are interested. Listen and repeat these expressions.

Great talking to you. Bye!   Cool!   Wow!   Oh, I see.   Really?

Here's my number.   Another soda?   All right.   Nice!

D Make it personal   *Let's party!* Role-play meeting new people at a party. Create a new identity if you want to.

1. Move around the class and ask a lot of questions.

> Hi, I'm … . Nice to meet you.   What do you do?   Do you live near here?

> Hello. My name's Richard VeryRich. Nice to meet you too.   I'm a banker and I work in the Bahamas.   Yes, I do. / No, I live on a yacht.

2. In pairs, remember all the people you met. Who has an unusual new identity?

41

Writing 3 A personal profile

*You don't know you're beautiful,
Oh, oh
That's what makes you beautiful.*

A ▶ 3.25 Read and complete Beth's profile with the words.

| a | Brazilian | daughters | has | in |
| lives | ~~old~~ | two | they're | works |

REGULAR PEOPLE, UNUSUAL FACTS

by Vicente Lucas, Brasília, Brazil

My sister Beth is a regular person in many ways. She's 48 years ___old___. She's divorced and she has two _____. Their names are Carol and Camila, and _____ 16 and 14. We're _____, from Rio de Janeiro, but Beth _____ in Argentina. She's _____ psychologist and she _____ in a school _____ Palermo, Buenos Aires. She's a happy person – very friendly and really popular. But _____ unusual facts about Beth: she doesn't have a car, but she _____ nine cats and four dogs in her apartment! She adores animals.

B Reread and answer questions 1–9.
1 How old is Beth?
2 Is she married?
3 How many children does she have?
4 How old are they?
5 Where's she from?
6 Where does she live?
7 What does she do?
8 Where does she work?
9 What's unusual about her?

C Read *Write it right!* Then, in the profile, circle:
- three examples of *but*
- 11 third person singular verbs
- an adjective intensified by *really*.

✓ **Write it right!**

Use *but* to contrast two ideas.
Remember the verb forms with -s for *he* or *she*.
Use *very* or *really* to intensify adjectives.
My brother is **really** intelligent.

D Think of a person you know. Complete 1–5 about him / her. What's unusual about him / her?
1 He / She has _____ in his / her house.
2 He / She lives with _____.
3 He / She is a(n) _____.
4 He / She works / studies in _____.
5 Other: _____.

E *Your turn!* Write a profile of the person in **D** for *Regular People, Unusual Facts*.

Before	Plan your answers to 1–9 in **B**. Compare with your sentences 1–5 in **D**.
While	Introduce your person and write the profile. Use *but* to contrast ideas, and *very* or *really* to intensify adjectives. Check the form of all your verbs.
After	Share your profile with the class. Who's the most unusual person?

3 Job interviews

1 Before watching

A Match photos 1–6 to these words. Which is not a job?
- [ ] barista
- [ ] filmmaker
- [ ] scientist
- [ ] customer
- [ ] manager
- [ ] songwriter

B Guess two jobs for August, Rory, Andrea, and Lucy.

I think August works with computers—he's an IT professional!

2 While watching

A Watch and check Andrea (An), August (Au), Genevieve (G), Lucy (L), or Rory (R).

	An	Au	G	L	R	
1						fixes Internet settings.
2						works with design.
3						works with robot programs.
4						directs movies.
5						fixes problems on computers.
6						works at ID Café.
7						is a filmmaker.
8						writes and sings songs.
9						serves coffee.

B Listen to Genevieve. Complete what she says.

I work here in this c_____. It's a big p_____. There are a _____ _____ tables. I'm a s_____ and a b_____. Baristas serve or make c_____, and serve it to the c_____. I work a lot, but this is not my p_____. I'm also a m_____ student at the university. And I'm a m_____, and s_____, and a s_____.

C Watch from 2:50 to 3:40. Number the words 1–9 in the order Rory says them.
- [ ] assistant manager
- [ ] expert
- [ ] fix
- [ ] problem
- [ ] settings
- [ ] signal
- [ ] strong
- [1] technician
- [ ] university

D Watch the complete video. True (T) or False (F)?
1. It's Andrea's office.
2. She works there with busy directors.
3. They work as interns or assistants to university professors.
4. Andrea works in design and fashion.
5. She doesn't work with clothes or furniture.
6. Her job is to combine materials and colors.
7. Lucy has two jobs.

3 After watching

A Complete 1–7 with *do*, *does*, *work* or *works*.
1. This is August. What _____ he do?
2. Where _____ you _____, and what _____ you do?
3. I _____ at home a lot and I _____ on robots.
4. Our computer signal _____.
5. We _____ with a lot of material for clothes.
6. _____ they work? Yeah, they _____.
7. That's what they _____.

B Complete the adjectives they use. Who says them?
1. Robots are s*pecial* and f_____!
2. Your work is really in_____.
3. Our computer signal is s_____.
4. That was g_____!
5. It's a very i_____ job.
6. The designers are very b_____.
7. Design is about e_____ taste and b_____ colors.

C What do the characters do? In pairs, ask and answer.

What does Andrea do? *She works with colors and clothes.*

D 🎤 **Make it personal** Role-play! In pairs, **A:** Imagine you have one of the jobs in **1A**. **B:** Interview A. Use adjectives from **3B**. Change roles.

What do you do? *I'm a songwriter.*

Really? That's great! What type of songs do you write?

4

4.1 Is there an ATM near here?

① Vocabulary Personal items

A ▶4.1 Match these items to photos 1–10. Then listen to Vero talking about the contents of her purse, and say which item is not in the photos.

- ☐ pills
- ☐ a comb /koʊm/
- ☐ an ID card
- ☐ a **lip**stick
- ☐ a **char**ger
- ☐ coins
- ☒ 1 an um**brel**la
- ☐ keys
- ☐ mints
- ☐ a **wal**let

B ▶4.2 Listen to, point to, and repeat items 1–10.

♪ This the part when I say I don't want it,
I'm stronger than I've been before,
This is the part when I break free.

4.1

2 Pronunciation /ɪ/, /iː/ and /ð/

A ▶4.3 Read and listen to the information. Then practice the examples.

> Be careful with /ɪ/ and /iː/.
> /ɪ/ Th**i**s is a l**i**pstick. It's p**i**nk.
> /iː/ Th**ese** are k**ey**s. Thr**ee** gr**ee**n k**ey**s.
> The *s* in *this* is pronounced /s/. The *s* in *these* is pronounced /z/.
> The *th* in *this, these,* and *there* is pronounced /ð/.

B ▶4.4 Listen to 1–5 and check /ɪ/ or /iː/. Listen again and repeat.

		/ɪ/	/iː/
1	Nick's sister has six children.	✓	
2	Repeat, please.		
3	Big pills and little mints.		
4	Think of six big things.		
5	Read and complete these forms.		

> **Common mistakes**
>
> ~~What's it?~~ this *(or What is it?)*
> These
> ~~This~~ are pens.

C ▶4.5 Play *Race the beep!* Look again at the photos in **1A**. Listen and say *This is a / These are* and the correct word before the beep.

1 This is an umbrella.   2 This is a wallet.

3 Grammar *There + be*

A Complete the grammar box with *There's* or *There are*.

Singular	Plural
_____ a charger on the table. _____ an ATM near my house.	_____ four candies in the box. _____ a lot of coins in my wallet.
_____ is the contraction of *There is*.	

→ **Grammar 4A** p.78

> **Common mistakes**
>
> There's 10 students in my class. → *are*
> ~~Have~~ keys on the table. → There are
> How many chairs ~~there are~~ in the office? → *are there*

B ▶4.6 Listen and follow the model. Practice the sentences.

> There's a book on the table. – pens   There are pens on the table.

C Complete with *there's, there are,* or *are there*.
1 How many students _____ in this class?
2 _____ pills in my backpack.
3 Look, _____ a purse on the seat!
4 _____ an umbrella in my car.
5 How many objects _____ on the table?
6 _____ eight candies in the box.

D 🔵 **Make it personal** Play *Memory test!* Close your books. In pairs, in two columns, remember all the items in the photos on p. 44. Which pair can remember the most?

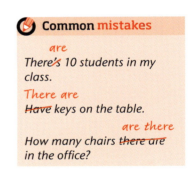

There's ...   There are ...
a hand   a lot of coins

45

4.2 Are those your books?

1 Listening

A ▶4.7 Look at the picture. Listen to Marty and Amy and answer 1–3.
1 What do they find?
2 Who opens it?
3 Guess six items they find in it.

I think there's a wallet in it.

| book | candies | cell phone | comb | flash drive | glasses |
| headphones | ID card | keys | pen | pills | wallet |

B ▶4.8 Listen to the rest of the conversation. What items do they find? How many correct guesses?

2 Grammar *this / that / these / those*

A ▶4.9 Match questions and pictures 1–4 to the answers. Listen, check, and repeat.

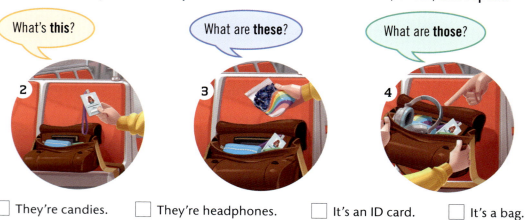

What's **that**? What's **this**? What are **these**? What are **those**?

☐ They're candies. ☐ They're headphones. ☐ It's an ID card. ☐ It's a bag.

B Singular or plural? Write S or P next to the questions in **A**. Then complete the grammar box with *that, these* and *those*.

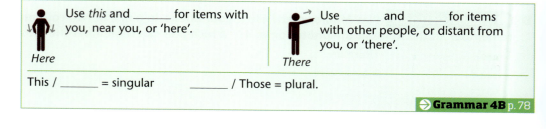

Use *this* and _____ for items with you, near you, or 'here'.
Here

Use _____ and _____ for items with other people, or distant from you, or 'there'.
There

This / _____ = singular   _____ / Those = plural.

➡ Grammar 4B p. 78

⚠ Common mistakes

that
What's ~~this~~?

46

♪ *I'm waiting for it, that green light, I want it,*
Oh, I wish I could get my things and just let go.

4.2

C ▶ 4.10 Complete with *this*, *these*, *that* or *those*. Listen, check, and repeat.

 1 _____ is my new phone.

 2 _____ are my books.

 3 What's _____?

 4 What are _____?

 5 Hey! _____'s my car.

 6 _____ are my children.

D ▶ 4.11 Listen and follow the model. Practice the sentences.

This – question   *What's this?*   *a wallet*   *It's a wallet.*

E 🗨 **Make it personal** In pairs, test your partner.
1 Show items you have with you, or point at photos in *your* book.

What's this?   *It's a pencil.*   *What are these?*   *They're keys.*

2 Point to items around the classroom or point at photos in *your partner's* book.

What's that?   *It's an eraser.*   *What are those?*   *They're windows.*

③ Vocabulary Colors

A ▶ 4.12 Match the colors to 1–10 in **B**. Listen, check, and repeat.

black   **blue**   **brown**   **green**   **gray**   **orange**   **pink**   **red**   **yellow**   **white**

B In pairs, ask and answer about 1–10.

 1
 2
 3
 4
 5
 6
 7   8
 9
 10

What's this?   *It's a black bike.*   *What are these?*   *They're green glasses.*

⚠ **Common mistake**
blue birds
They're ~~birds blues~~.

C 🗨 **Make it personal** In pairs, test your partner using items in the classroom. How many questions can you ask and answer correctly in five minutes?

What color are those chairs?   *They're gray. What color is the whiteboard?*   *It's white!*

4.3 What things do you lose?

1 Reading

A ▶4.13 Read the article and match statements 1–4 to pictures a–d. Guess the pronunciation of the pink-stressed words. Then listen and check.

a

b

c

d

Japanese honesty

(1) Hundreds of people lose personal items in big cities every day, (2) and hundreds of people find these items. In Tokyo, with a population of 33 million, (3) officers at the Lost and Found Center collect hundreds of things every day and catalogue them in a database. (4) The result is 72% of the items are returned to the happy owners! What honest people! Is your country similar or different?

B Reread the question at the end of the text. Choose your answer(s) from 1–5. In pairs, compare. Do you agree?

1. I think it's the same here.
2. I don't think people are honest here.
3. People are honest here too.
4. People don't return items here.
5. Lost and Found centers don't work here.

I (don't) agree with number 1.   *It depends.*

2 Vocabulary Plural nouns (3)

A ▶4.14 Read and listen. Then match photos 1–6 to the underlined words.

Transport for London (TfL) finds 400,000 lost items on the London trains, buses, and taxis every year. The usual things are ID cards, wallets, cell phones, and keys, but what about the unusual items? Officers find false teeth, toothbrushes, suitcases, personal diaries, and even fish!

48

♪ You're dangerous cause you're honest, You're dangerous 'cause you don't know what you want.

4.3

B Complete the information with the underlined words from **A**.

Most plurals = noun + s	Some plurals have special spellings.	Some plurals are irregular.
one key, two keys one umbrella, two umbrellas 1 _____	• Nouns ending in consonant + *y*, change *-y* to *-ies*. one candy, two candies 2 _____ • Nouns ending in *-sh, -ch, -s, -z* or *-x*, add *-es*. one watch, two watches 3 _____ 4 _____ Pronounce *-es* as an extra syllable /ɪz/.	one man, two men one woman, two women one child, two children one person, two people one tooth, some ⁵ _____ one fish, some ⁶ _____

➔ **Grammar 4C** p. 78

C In pairs, test your partner. Take turns saying a noun. Your partner says and spells the plural noun.

› candy   › candies – C-A-N-D-I-E-S

D 🗣 **Make it personal** What things do you lose? In pairs, compare.   › I lose my phone and my keys every day!

⚠ **Common mistakes**
I have two ~~camera~~. *cameras*
They are red~~s~~ pens.

③ Listening Telling the time

A ▶ 4.15 Listen and match conversations 1–6 to the correct clock. Listen again and repeat the times.

› Excuse me, what time is it, please?   › It's seven forty-five.

08:10 ☐   04:30 ☐   07:45 [1]

11:50 ☐   02:00 ☐   05:15 ☐

B ▶ 4.16 Listen and write the six times. In pairs, compare. Any differences?

C 🗣 **Make it personal** Write more times for your partner to practice saying.

› What time is it?   › It's two fifteen.

⚠ **Common mistake**
time is it / 's the time
What ~~hours are~~?

D 🗣 **Make it personal** Write five times between 11:05 and 11:55. Listen to your teacher and play ***Bingo!***

49

4.4 What time do you get up?

1 Reading and vocabulary Typical days

A ▶4.17 Read and listen to Leroy's blog entry. Match pictures a–j to the **bold** phrases.

Search 🔍   HOME   ABOUT   ARCHIVE   SUBSCRIBE

My typical day
Hi guys! Hope we can find a good time to chat and game.

I do virtually the same things every day. I **get up** ☐ at seven o'clock and **check my phone** ☐. You know, social media, read the news … I **have breakfast** ☐ at about 7:40. Then it's time to go to school. I **leave home** ☐ at eight o'clock (my bus leaves at 8:10).

I start school at nine o'clock, **have lunch** ☐ at 12:45, and finish at 3:30. After school, I **go home,** ☐ or **go to the gym** ☐. I'm free from 5 to 7:45.

I **have dinner** ☐ with my family around eight. After dinner, I relax or **study** ☐ – or play video games with you! Finally, I **go to bed** ☐ at around midnight.

What about you? Is your typical day similar or very different? When is a good time to play?

a

b   c

f

g   h

B Reread. True (T) or False (F)?
1 Leroy wants to play video games.
2 His typical day is different every day.
3 He reads a newspaper every morning.
4 He goes to the gym every day.
5 He goes to bed at twelve o'clock.

C In pairs. A: Cover the text in **A** and use the pictures to describe Leroy's typical day. B: Help A as necessary. Then change roles.

> He gets up at seven o'clock and he checks his phone.

D Is your typical day similar to or different than Leroy's?

> I get up at six o'clock!   I check my phone at breakfast.   I go to bed at around one thirty!

E 🔵 **Make it personal** In pairs, take turns asking and answering about your typical day. Use the pictures in **A**. How many differences?

> What time do you get up?   What time do you go to school?
> I get up at 6:30 every morning.   I go to school at 7:45.

🎵 No one knows about you, about you,
And you're making the typical me
break my typical rules,
It's true, I'm a sucker for you.

4.4

ⓘ Common mistakes

have
I ~~take the~~ breakfast / lunch / dinner at …
He gets up at ~~the~~ 7:30 ~~o'clock~~.
W
~~At~~ what time do you go to work?

d

e

i

j

4.5 How do you pronounce *meme* in English?

ID Skills Pronouncing and spelling cognates

A How many "technology" words do you know in English? Make a list.

I know a lot ... computer, radio, cell phone ...   *And what about charger?*

B Read the article and underline any words from your list in **A**. Are 1–4 True (T) or False (F)?

> **Common mistake**
>
> There are ̂a lot of apps on my cell phone.

HOME   ABOUT   ARCHIVE   SUBSCRIBE

INFORMATION TECHNOLOGY

Information technology (IT) is responsible for a lot of new English words, and many of these are now international. *Electronic mail*, for example, is *email*, and *applications* (computer and software programs for mobile devices) are *apps*. Other words—*blog*, *gigabyte*, *smartphone*, *Wi-Fi* and, of course, *Internet*—are now common internationally. Social networks contribute with *Facebook*, *Twitter* (and *tweet*—the noun and verb for a post on *Twitter*), and others. And old words get new meanings too—a *tablet*, for example, is not just another word for a *pill*!

1. Many new words in English are from IT.
2. There aren't a lot of English IT words in other languages.
3. The words *email* and *apps* are abbreviations.
4. There's only one meaning for the word *tablet*.

C ▶ 4.18 Listen and reread. In pairs, do 1–3.
1. Practice the pink-stressed words, and words in italics. Find at least ten cognates.
2. Say which of the cognates have the same spelling in your language.
3. Practice the final consonant sound in the eight highlighted words.

D ▶ 4.19 Listen to a conversation and note the six technology words you hear.

E ▶ 4.19 Listen again. Which tablet is it, a, b, or c?

F 🅐 **Make it personal** *Spelling test!* In pairs, take turns asking the spelling of the cognates in the article in **B**. One point for each correct answer. Be careful with pronunciation!

How do you spell technology?   *T - E - C - H ...*

What color is your wallet?

*Tell me somethin', girl
Are you happy in this modern world?
Or do you need more?
Is there somethin' else you're searchin' for?*

4.5

ID in Action Asking about lost property

A ▶4.20 Listen to a conversation. Where exactly are the people? What is the problem? Choose the correct wallet from 1–4.

B ▶4.20 Listen again and number the sentences in the order you hear them, 1–8.

All the money for my vacation!	☐	OK, and what color is the wallet?	☐
Can I help you?	☐	Yesterday?	☐
Do you know where?	☐	Now, let's see what there is in the system.	☐
I lost my wallet.	☐	It's very big.	☐

C In pairs, complete this part of the Lost and Found report.

D Read AS 4.20 on p. 86. Read to check you have all the correct information in **C**. Do you think the man will be lucky?

E In pairs, practice the dialogue using AS 4.20 on p. 86. Copy the intonation. Then change roles.

F Practice again without the script. Use only the information in **B**.

G 🅐 **Make it personal** In pairs, role-play a conversation at Lost and Found. Then change roles. Be creative!

A: Lose an item.
B: Complete the form in **C**.

Excuse me, is this Lost and Found?

Yes, can I help you?

Yes, I lost my cell phone.

53

Writing 4 A description

Yeah, I left my wallet in El Segundo
Left my wallet in El Segundo
Left my wallet in El Segundo I gotta get it,
I got-got ta get it.

A ▶ 4.21 Read Kylee's lost property report. Choose the correct bag 1–3.

LOST PROPERTY REPORT

Fares   Help & contact   More ˅

Name: Kylee Hurst
Email: k.hurst04@usanet.us
Date lost: 02/16/2020

Location:
I lost my bag in Union Station, in the Mexican restaurant or at the Mini Golf.

Description of object:
It's a big green bag. It's really important because my wallet is in it, with my ID, credit card and about $50 too! There's a very expensive tablet in it too! And there are a lot of pens, a notebook and a new blue sweater. Please help me find it because my mom is not very happy with me at the moment!

B True (T) or False (F)?
1. Kylee lost her bag in an airport.
2. She knows exactly where she lost her bag.
3. There's money in the wallet in her bag.
4. Kylee mentions a total of nine items that are in her bag.
5. Kylee's mom and dad are unhappy with her.

C Read *Write it right!* In the report, (circle) two examples of:
- reasons introduced by *because*
- *too* to give extra information
- two adjectives before a noun.

✓ Write it right!

Use *because* to introduce a reason.
*I go to classes **because** I want to learn English.*
Use *too* at the end of a sentence to give additional information.
*I study French **too**.*
To describe a noun using two adjectives, put them **before** the noun.
*I have a **great new app** on my phone.*

D Imagine you lost a bag in Union Station. Answer 1–8.
1. Is the bag big or small?
2. Is it new or old?
3. What color is it?
4. Where and when did you lose it?
5. What items in it are really important?
6. Are there other items in the bag?
7. Are these items new or old? Cheap or expensive? Colors?
8. Why is it important to find the bag today?

E 🎧 **Make it personal** Write a description of your bag for a lost property report.

Before	Use your answers to the questions in **D**. Follow Kylee's model carefully.
While	Include *because* and a reason. Include *too* and extra information. Use two adjectives for the "really important" items.
After	Share your report with a partner. Check her / his report. Send it to your teacher.

4 In the bag

 Café

1 Before watching

A 🔴 **Make it personal** In pairs, list the items you have with you today. Compare with the class. Score one point for each item that only you have.

Apartment keys, my electricity bill ...

B Rory and August have new school supplies. Guess five items in their bags.

I don't know. Maybe pens?

2 While watching

A True (T) or false (F)? Watch to check.
1 Rory's helping because Daniel's not at home.
2 August's cat's name is Garfield.
3 There are three folders.
4 There's a blackboard in one bag.
5 Rory's hungry for a pizza.
6 Daniel keeps a menu in the kitchen.
7 Rory's books are in the kitchen.
8 August's cell phone is on the sofa.

B Number the events 1–7 in the order you hear them.
___ Rory puts his bag on the table.
___ The cat makes a sound.
___ There are many school supplies in the bags.
___ August looks for his cell phone in his room.
___ August and Rory hear the cat.
___ August is hungry.
___ Rory and August sit on the sofa.

C Check the colors you think they mention. Listen again to check, and write the numbers you hear.

Colors	Notebooks	Pens	Erasers	Folders
Black				
Blue				
Green				
Pink				
Purple				
Red				
Yellow				
White				

3 After watching

A Match expressions 1–7 to each situation.

Expressions	Near or with you	Far from you
1 Somewhere over there!		
2 I have two of them right here.		
3 That's where Daniel keeps it.		
4 No, it's not in there.		
5 Maybe over there?		
6 There it is!		
7 And here's my cell phone.		

B Complete 1–6 with *this*, *that*, *that's* or *these*.
1 _____ bags are really full.
2 Is _____ yours? What's _____ for?
3 _____ yours. It's for pens, pencils and erasers. And _____ is a bill organizer.
4 And in _____ bag, there is a whiteboard.
5 OK. _____ bag is empty! And my stomach is empty too.
6 It's in the folder in the kitchen. _____ where Daniel keeps it.

C Complete 1–4 with *'s*, *is* or *are*.
1 There _____ so many school supplies in these bags.
2 When there _____ a sale, you've got to buy!
3 There _____ two notebooks.
4 And in this bag there _____ a whiteboard.

D 🔴 **Make it personal** In pairs, ask and answer about pets. Do you have a pet? What's its name?

I have a cat. Her name is Princess.

There are two pets in my house. We have a cat and a dog.

R2 Grammar and vocabulary

A **Picture dictionary.** Cover the words on these pages and remember.

page	
32	10 jobs
33	16 more jobs
34	15 family members
36	9 places of work
41	9 conversation expressions
44	10 personal objects
47	10 colors
48	6 plural nouns
49	6 times
50–51	a typical day

B **Make it personal** Add *do* or *does* in the correct place. In pairs, ask and answer.
1 Where you live?
2 your father have a job?
3 What your mother do?
4 you live alone, or with other people?
5 you have children?
6 When your family go to bed?

C Match jobs 1–5 to the places. Then ask questions to test a partner.
1 a pharmacist — an office
2 a lawyer — a restaurant
3 a sales clerk — a school
4 a teacher — a drugstore
5 a server — a store

Where does a server work?
In a restaurant.

D ▶R2.1 Complete Meg's description of her family with *this, that, these, those,* or *they*.

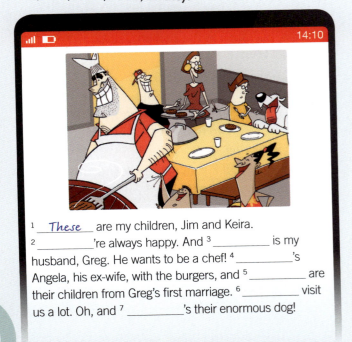

1 _These_ are my children, Jim and Keira.
2 _____ 're always happy. And 3 _____ is my husband, Greg. He wants to be a chef! 4 _____ 's Angela, his ex-wife, with the burgers, and 5 _____ are their children from Greg's first marriage. 6 _____ visit us a lot. Oh, and 7 _____ 's their enormous dog!

E **Make it personal** Circle the correct words in 1–5. Then make the sentences true for you.
1 My brother **work** / **works** **at** / **in** a small office.
2 There **is** / **are** only one child in my family.
3 My aunt **don't** / **doesn't** live with **your** / **her** son.
4 My sister **have** / **has** two children, but she **don't** / **doesn't** have a dog or a cat.
5 My girlfriend **don't** / **doesn't** have siblings.

F Write the plurals. In pairs, describe the photos in units 3 and 4 using *There is / are*. Talk about the number of items in the photos.

diary _____   fish _____
dog _____   tooth _____
pill _____   toothbrush _____
shoe _____   bus _____

There are a lot of pills in the photo on page 44.
Yes, and there's a hairdresser on page 32.

G **Make it personal** In groups, complete the form about a famous character in a popular TV show or movie. Can the class guess who it is?

Age:
Nationality:
Marital status:
Family:
Occupation:
Place of work:
Place of residence:
Your opinion about her / him:
Imagine one or two things she / he does on a typical day:

He's around 30 years old, he's from ...
He has a wife and two children ...

H Correct the mistakes. Check your answers in units 3 and 4.

Common mistakes
1 She's teacher. She work in Manaus. (2 mistakes)
2 Do you has childrens? (2 mistakes)
3 My fathers live in downtown. (2 mistakes)
4 You work in home? (2 mistakes)
5 Ana get ups at the seven in the morning. (2 mistakes)
6 My boyfriend gos to the bed late. (2 mistakes)
7 John don't live with his mother, he lives with her wife. (2 mistakes)
8 Of what color are this pencil? (2 mistakes)
9 Have a book in the table. (2 mistakes)
10 What time it is? (1 mistake)

Skills practice

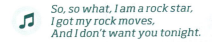

*So, so what, I am a rock star,
I got my rock moves,
And I don't want you tonight.*

R2

A ▶R2.2 Listen to an introduction to a radio interview with a diplomat and answer 1–3.

1. What's the diplomat's name? _____
2. Where's she from? _____
3. Where does she live? _____

B ▶R2.3 Listen to the complete interview and check the questions you hear.

- [ ] Where are you from in Brazil?
- [ ] How old are you?
- [ ] How old is your husband?
- [ ] Is Antonio from Rio too?
- [ ] What does he do?
- [ ] Where does he work?
- [ ] Do you have children?
- [ ] What's his name?
- [ ] How old is he?
- [ ] Where do you live here in Bogotá?
- [ ] What do you think of Bogotá and Colombia?
- [ ] What's your favorite thing about Colombia?

C ▶R2.3 Do you remember the answers? Circle the correct option. Listen again to check.

1. Rosa **is** / **isn't** from Rio de Janeiro.
2. She's **33** / **43** years old.
3. Her husband **is** / **isn't** Brazilian.
4. He's a **diplomat** / **teacher**.
5. He works at **home** / **downtown**.
6. Their **son** / **daughter** is four years old.
7. They **live** / **don't live** in a nice area.
8. Rosa **thinks** / **doesn't think** Colombia and Bogotá are very nice.
9. Her favorite thing about Colombia is the **fruit** / **music**.

D In pairs, role-play the interview. Use the questions in **B** and the information in **C**.

E Read and complete this blog extract with *there's* or *there are*. Read and say the 12 cognate adjectives.

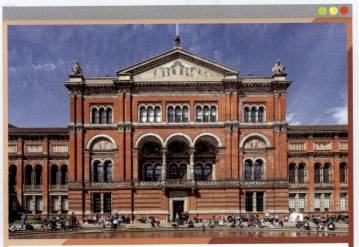

If you're in London, a visit to the Victoria and Albert museum—"the V&A"—is <u>essential</u>. And no, it isn't a museum about Queen Victoria and her husband, Albert! It's the greatest collection of <u>historical</u> and <u>contemporary</u> <u>decorative</u> arts and design in the world.

Situated in <u>glamorous</u> Kensington, _____ <u>magnificent</u> rooms and <u>ultra-modern</u> galleries. In total, _____ 145 galleries, but, with over 4.5 million objects, not all of the V&A's treasures are exhibited every day.

The V&A is incredibly <u>diverse</u>. _____ art from every continent, and _____ <u>fantastic</u> examples of every <u>human</u> activity—fashion, jewelry, ceramics, sculpture, architecture, photography, paintings, and toys. Plus, _____ the <u>famous</u> Great Bed of Ware, constructed in 1590, and big enough for eight people! It's mentioned in Shakespeare's play, *Twelfth Night* (1601)! _____ <u>marvelous</u> clothes from celebrities too, old and new, from rock stars to royals.
The V&A teaches you a lot and, best of all, entry is free!

F Reread. True (T) or false (F)? Would you like to go to the V&A museum?

1. The V&A is a museum about the royal family.
2. There isn't any modern art in the museum.
3. It's impossible to see all the V&A's collection in one day.
4. There aren't any objects from Asia.
5. There's an item from Shakespeare's house.
6. Many famous people's possessions are there.
7. It's expensive to go to the V&A museum.

G 🅐 **Make it personal** **Question time.**

In pairs, practice asking and answering the 12 lesson titles in units 3 and 4. Use the book map on p. 2–3. Where possible, ask follow-up questions, too. Can you comfortably ask and answer all the questions?

What do you do?

I'm unemployed. But I study English every day, and I want to work in tourism.

5

5.1 Do you drink a lot of coffee?

1 Vocabulary Meals, food (1), and drinks

I love dinner. It's my favorite meal.

A ▶5.1 Match photos 1–4 to these sentences. Listen to check.
What is your favorite meal of the day?

- [ ] I eat and drink this for **dinner**.
- [ ] We usually have this for **lunch**.
- [ ] Americans eat this for **breakfast**.
- [ ] This is only **a snack**.

Common mistakes

~~do~~
What ^do you have for ~~the~~ lunch?

B ▶5.2 Match items a–l in the photo to these words. Listen, check, and repeat.

[ ] **cof**fee	[ ] **veg**etables	[ ] cheese /tʃi:z/	[ ] milk
[ ] fruit /fru:t/	[ ] beans	[ ] eggs	[ ] **or**ange juice /dʒu:s/
[ ] tea	[ ] bread /bred/	[ ] meat	[ ] soft drinks

C 🎧 **Make it personal** What do you have for breakfast / lunch / dinner?
What do you have for a snack? Ask and answer in pairs, then tell the class.

Do you have eggs for breakfast? *No, I don't. I don't have time in the morning.*

58

♪ Cause I don't care, when I'm with my baby, yeah,
All the bad things disappear,
And you're making me feel like maybe I am somebody.

5.1

2 Pronunciation Silent letters

A ▶5.3 Be careful with "silent" letters. Listen and cross out the silent letters in these words. Listen again and repeat.

apple   bread   breakfast   cheese   fruit   juice   vegetables

B ▶5.4 Listen and write the sentences. In pairs, practice saying them.

3 Listening

A ▶5.5 Listen to a couple talking about their meals. Answer 1–3.
1 Which three items in **1B** don't they mention?
2 What do they eat for breakfast and lunch?
3 Do they eat or drink any items that are bad for you?

B 🅼 **Make it personal** In your opinion, which food and drinks in **1B** are good or bad for you? In pairs, compare.

I think … is / are bad for you.   *I agree. / I disagree. I think … is / are good for you.*

> **Common mistakes**
>
> ~~The~~ soft drinks are bad for you.
> ~~The~~ milk is good for you.
> My favorite meal is ~~the~~ breakfast.
> Don't use *the* with nouns to talk about things generically.

4 Reading

A In pairs, read the nutrition tip and try to pronounce the pink-stressed words.

B Reread and pronounce the highlighted letters /ʃ/ like *shark* and *shorts*.

C ▶5.6 Listen and reread to check. Do you agree with the conclusion?

🍴 NUTRITION TIP

We all know that milk, beans, vegetables, fruit, and water are good for us. And other foods are "bad"—soft drinks, white sugar, alcohol, for example. But items like bread, cheese, eggs, meat, coffee, and tea are controversial. Doctors, scientists, and nutritionists all have different opinions and say different things. Are these foods and drinks good or bad?

We say it all depends on quantity. Life is short! We say "Yes" to moderation, but "No" to exaggeration. What do you think?

I agree. Moderation is good.   *I disagree. I think bread and meat are bad for you, and the planet!*

D ▶5.7 Listen to an interview. True (T) or False (F)?
Does Jack have generally good or bad habits?
1 Jack is vegetarian.   2 Jack drinks a lot of coffee.   3 He doesn't like bread.

E 🅼 **Make it personal** In pairs, ask and answer about your eating habits. What do you eat and drink? Do you generally have good or bad habits?

Do you eat (a lot of) vegetables?   *Well, for breakfast I eat … and I drink …*

59

5.2 What's your favorite food?

1 Vocabulary Food (2)

A ▶5.8 Match photos a–p to these words. In pairs, guess their pronunciation. All the highlighted letters are pronounced /ə/ like *bananas* and *pajamas*. Listen, check, and repeat.

- [ ] bananas
- [ ] beef
- [ ] carrots
- [ ] chicken /tʃɪkɪn/
- [ ] Chinese
- [ ] fish
- [ ] French fries
- [ ] grapes
- [ ] hot dogs
- [ ] Italian
- [ ] Japanese
- [ ] lettuce /letɪs/
- [ ] oranges
- [ ] pizza
- [ ] potatoes
- [ ] tomatoes

B **Make it personal** Cover the words in **A**. In pairs, ask and answer *Do you like …?* using the photos. Any differences between you?

Do you like grapes?   *Yes, I do!*   *I don't like grapes. I prefer wine!*

♪ *I love it when you go crazy,*
You take all my inhibitions,
Baby, there's nothing holding me back.

5.2

2 Listening

A ▶5.9 Read the forum and match food groups 1–5 on p. 60 to the posts. Listen to the interviews to check. Are you similar to the people?

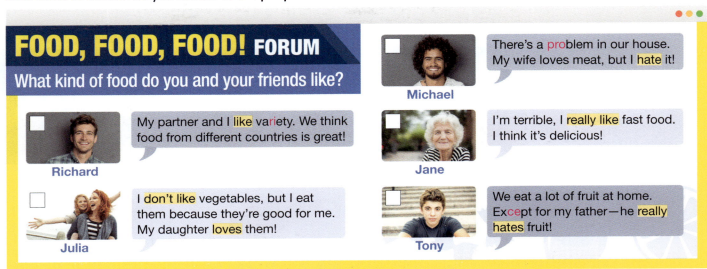

FOOD, FOOD, FOOD! FORUM
What kind of food do you and your friends like?

Richard: My partner and I **like** variety. We think food from different countries is great!

Julia: I **don't like** vegetables, but I eat them because they're good for me. My daughter **loves** them!

Michael: There's a **pro**blem in our house. My wife loves meat, but I **hate** it!

Jane: I'm terrible, I **really like** fast food. I think it's delicious!

Tony: We eat a lot of fruit at home. Except for my father—he **really hates** fruit!

B 🔔 Make it personal Do you know three more food or drink words in English? In pairs, compare.

I know mangoes. It's similar to Portuguese!

Common mistakes
I like ~~very much~~ the chicken.
He like~~s~~ the banana.
       doesn't
She ~~not like~~ the fruit.

3 Grammar like / love / don't like / hate

A Complete the scale with the **highlighted** phrases in **2A**.

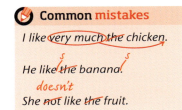

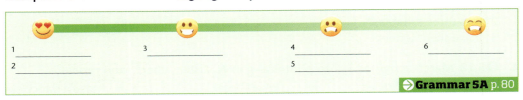

1 _____   3 _____   4 _____   6 _____
2 _____   5 _____

➔ Grammar 5A p. 80

B True (T) or False (F) for you? Change the verb in the false sentences to make them true.
1 I like bread and cheese.
2 I love pizza.
3 I really hate black coffee.
4 I don't like fast food.
5 I really like Italian restaurants.
6 I hate fish.

C ▶5.10 Listen and follow the model. Practice the sentences.

I don't like Italian food. – he   He doesn't like Italian food.

D 🔔 Make it personal Complete the sentences for you. In pairs, compare. Any similarities or differences?

❶ I love _____ and _____.
❷ I like _____, but I don't like _____.
❸ I really hate _____.
❹ I really like _____.
❺ My best friend likes _____, but he / she hates _____.
❻ In _____, people usually eat _____ on weekends.

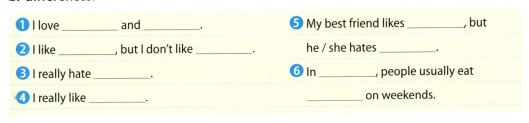

What kind of food do you love?
I love fish, but I really hate chicken!

5.3 What do you usually do on Friday evenings?

1 Vocabulary Days of the week and free-time activities

A ▶5.11 Complete the days on the calendar. Listen to the poem to check.

- a **Mon**day
- b **Tues**day
- c **Wednes**day
- d **Thurs**day
- e _ _ iday
- f _ _ _ urday
- g _ _ nday

I love Wednesdays and Sundays—I watch soccer on TV!

For me, it's Friday. The weekend starts!

B ▶5.11 Listen again and repeat the days. Then answer 1–5.

Which day(s) …
1. have a capital letter?
2. has three syllables?
3. have silent letters?
4. have the same first letter in your language?
5. are your two favorite days?

C ▶5.12 Match activities 1–7 to photos a–g in **A**. Listen, check, and repeat.
1. ☐ go to the movies
2. ☐ go to the mall
3. ☐ go to church
4. ☐ play soccer
5. ☐ watch TV
6. ☐ take a dance class
7. ☐ cook

2 Reading

A ▶5.13 Read the posts and match the people to three of the photos a–g in **1A**. Then listen and complete the posts with the days of the week.

WEEKENDS AROUND THE WORLD – WHAT DO YOU DO ON WEEKENDS?

MAYA GARCÍA
Here in Barranquilla, Colombia, sports like cycling, swimming, and a lot of others are very popular! I'm usually very active on weekends. I play soccer or baseball with my friends on ¹_____ morning, and in the afternoon we play video games or go to the gym.

LEE KON
We live in Seoul, South Korea, and we never stay home on ²_____ or ³_____ evenings. We see friends on the weekend. We sometimes go to a restaurant, or go to the movies. In Seoul, there are a lot of movie theaters, and you can to go to the movies 24 hours a day!

GIL LÓPEZ
I'm from Madrid in Spain. I always go to church on ⁴_____ during the day, but in the evening, I stay home. I listen to music, or I read a book. It depends how tired I am.

🎵 *I wanna rock n roll all night and party every day.*

5.3

B Reread and complete 1–5 with *on*, *on the*, or *in the*.
1 _____ weekend   2 _____ weekends   3 _____ Monday
4 _____ Monday afternoon   5 _____ morning / afternoon / evening

C Find and circle nine more free-time activities in the posts in **A**.

D 🅐 **Make it personal** Study Common mistakes, then, in pairs, compare your weekends with the posts. Any big differences or similarities?

I don't go to the gym on Saturday.   *I go to the movies on weekends.*

3 Grammar Frequency adverbs

Common mistakes

We take a class ~~in~~ *on* Friday evening.
I go to ~~the~~ school ~~the~~ *on M*onday.
I listen ~~/~~ *to* music ~~all the days~~ *every day*.
~~Usually~~ *I usually* stay ~~in~~ home after ~~the~~ work.

A Look at the examples in the grammar box and circle the correct word in the rule. Reread the posts in **2A** and underline the frequency adverbs.

100%	I **always** go to the gym on Tuesday.
	We **usually** eat in a restaurant on weekends.
	We **sometimes** go to a bar in the evening.
0%	My friends and I **never** stay home on Saturday night.

Frequency adverbs usually go immediately **before** / **after** the main verb.

➡ **Grammar 5B** p. 80

B ▶5.14 Put the words in 1–5 in order to make sentences. Listen, check, and repeat. Are they true for you?
1 I / remember / to / usually / my / homework / do / class / before
   I usually remember to do my homework before class!
2 the movies / we / go / always / Friday / evening / on / to
3 read / I / the / sometimes / on / a / book / weekend
4 my family and I / Sunday / go / to / a / restaurant / on / usually
5 never / I / watch / Saturday / on / TV / morning

C ▶5.15 Listen and follow the model. Practice the sentences.

We play soccer on Friday. – Always   *We always play soccer on Friday.*   *Never*   *We never play soccer on Friday.*

D 🅐 **Make it personal** In pairs, ask, answer, and complete the table for your partner. Compare with another pair. Any big differences?

What do you usually do on weekends?

	Morning	Afternoon	Evening
Friday			
Saturday			
Sunday			

What do you usually do on Friday evening?   *I sometimes watch TV.*

63

5.4 Do you like Rihanna's music?

1 Listening

1. Ryan Gosling's movies
2. Stephen Colbert's show
3. James Bond's car
4. _____'s autobiography
5. _____'s racket
6. _____'s tattoo
7. _____'s trophy
8. _____'s house

A Read and complete the newsfeed entries with photo captions 1–3.

ENTERTAINMENT NEWS   Friday, April 17

☐ Michelle Obama on (2) this Friday.
☐ People all over the world admire (___), the Aston Martin DB5.
☐ Collection of (___) released as a boxset this weekend.

B ▶5.16 Listen to two friends talking about the entertainment news. Which photos do they mention? Do you agree with their opinions?

2 Grammar Possessive 's

A Read the grammar box and circle the correct answer in 1 and 2. Then match the people to their possessions in photos 4–8 in **1A**.

Use a name or a noun + 's for the possessive. I like Ryan Gosling's movies. My sister's car is red.	's can mean *is* or the possessive. 1 He's my brother. ('s = *is* / the *possessive*) 2 Tessa's mother works downtown. ('s = *is* / the *possessive*)

→ **Grammar 5C** p. 80

The U.S. President   Naomi Osaka   Michelle Obama
The soccer team   Calvin Harris

B ▶5.17 Listen and follow the model. Practice the phrases.

The movies of Ryan Gosling   Ryan Gosling's movies   *Possessive adjective*   His movies

C 🎧 **Make it personal** Write the names of three people in your family and the first letter of a possession for each person. In pairs, guess who it is and what the possession is.

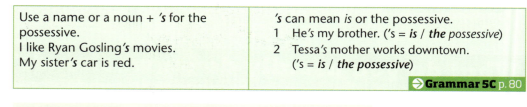

Jorge, B.   Is Jorge your brother's name?   *Yes, it is!*   Is it Jorge's bottle? Banana? Bus?

♫ Only hate the road when you're missing home,
Only know you love her when you let her go,
And you let her go.

5.4

③ Grammar Object pronouns

A ▶5.18 Read the questions and ⓒircle the correct words. Listen, check, and repeat.

Questions ❓		Answers ➕ ➖	
What do you think of	Lady Gaga?	I love	she / him / her.
	the *Twilight Saga* **books**?	I (don't) like	it / them / he.
Do you like	LeBron James?		him / her / he.
	Mexican **food**?		it / they / them.

→ Grammar 5C p. 80

B ▶5.16 Complete the dialogue with object pronouns. Listen again to check.
- **Ella** Look! A collection of Ryan Gosling's movies are on boxset this weekend.
- **Luke** Really? That's great! I like ¹_____ a lot. He's a great actor. I think his movies are excellent.
- **Ella** Hmmm. I don't like ²_____ much.
- **Luke** What?! They're fantastic! And what's on TV?
- **Ella** Do you like Stephen Colbert's show?
- **Luke** Yes, I do. I really like ³_____. Why?
- **Ella** Well, Michelle Obama is on his show tonight.
- **Luke** Michelle Obama? Again? I think Colbert loves ⁴_____!
- **Ella** Well, the show is about Michelle's new book.
- **Luke** Her autobiography? Oh, maybe I can read ⁵_____.

C ▶5.19 Listen and follow the model. Practice the sentences.

I like Adele.   I like her.   I never watch American movies.   I never watch them.

D Complete the mini dialogues. Then in pairs, practice them.
1. **A** This is my car. Do you like _____?
   B It's great! I like _____ very much!
2. **A** What do you think of the *Star Wars* movies? Do you like _____?
   B No, I really hate _____. I think they're boring.
3. **A** I love Billy Eilish. What do you think of _____?
   B She's fantastic. I like _____ a lot.
4. **A** What do you think of Chris Evans?
   B I like _____ a lot. I think he's an excellent actor.

E 🟢 **Make it personal** In pairs, ask for and share opinions about these celebrities and your favorite brands of the items in the photos.

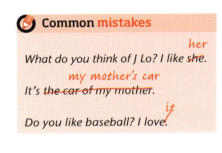

⚠️ **Common mistakes**

What do you think of J Lo? I like ~~she~~ her.

It's ~~the car of my mother~~ my mother's car.

Do you like baseball? I love. it

Do you like McDonald's burgers?

Yes, I like them a lot but I prefer Burger King burgers.

5.5 Do you eat a lot of fast food?

ID Skills Noticing sound-spelling combinations

A ▶5.20 What food can you see in photos a–d? Listen, read, and match the photos to restaurant recommendations 1–4.

 a
 b
 c
 d

1 Jane
Check out the cheeseburgers at this place. Great meat, delicious cheese, and amazing mayonnaise. I really recommend them.
★★★★★

2 Rick
I don't usually like ice cream, except for this one. I love their double chocolate cones. My sister likes the vanilla one with mango sauce!
★★★★☆

3 Viv
They open at six a.m. and I come here for breakfast every day! The fresh fruit salad with yogurt is fantastic. Their exotic juices are incredible too!
★★★★☆

4 Yuri
On weekends, my girlfriend and I always eat here. Their hot dogs and French fries are the best in the city, and the portions are very generous too!
★★★★★

Was this review helpful?

B Reread the recommendations in **A**. True (T) or False (F)? Correct the false sentences.
1 Jane likes cheeseburgers.
2 Rick likes vanilla ice cream.
3 Viv doesn't usually have breakfast at home.
4 Viv really likes fruit.
5 Yuri and his girlfriend eat hot dogs on Mondays.

C ▶5.21 Look at the pictures and say the pairs of words. Write the underlined words from **A** under the correct picture. Listen to check.

 dʒ
 b
 v
 r
 j

generous   _____   _____   _____   _____
_____   _____   _____   _____   _____
_____   _____   _____   _____   _____

D In pairs, say the five other consonant pairs marked **P** and **S** in the Sounds and usual spellings chart on p.82–83. Read the example words under the chart and notice the different spellings.

E Make it personal Story time! Write a sentence with one of the consonant pairs in **C** or **D**. Challenge the class to pronounce it perfectly!

> The vet drives a van.   A red rock on the road to Rio.

Anything to drink?

🎵 *Anything you want, you got it.*
Anything you need, you got it.
Anything at all, you got it. Baby!

5.5

a

b

c

Remember words and expressions with their opposites or associations.
For example:
  For here? – To go?
  Yes, please. – No, thanks.
  large – small
  with – without
  eat – drink
  ice – lemon
  cream – sugar

Common mistakes

~~Anything for drink?~~ *to*

~~For here or for go?~~ *to*

ID in Action Ordering food

A ▶5.22 What do they order? Listen and match conversations 1 and 2 with two of food trays a–c.

B ▶5.23 Match questions 1–5 to the answers. Listen, check, and repeat.

1 Can I help you?   ☐ A tea, please.
2 Anything to drink?   ☐ Large, please.
3 Large, medium, or small?   [1] A hot dog, please.
4 Cream and sugar?   ☐ No, thanks.
5 Anything else?   ☐ Just sugar, please.

C ▶5.24 Circle the correct words. Listen to check. In pairs, cover all the words and practice the dialogue.

ATTENDANT	CUSTOMER
Can I help you?	A hamburger and French fries, **please / thanks**.
Anything to **eat / drink?**	**A / An** cola.
Large, medium, or small?	**Medium. / Small.**
With ice?	**Yes, please. / No, thanks.**
Anything **else / to drink?**	**Yes, please. / No, thanks.**
For here or to go?	**For here. / To go.**
That's $12.95.	There you are. **Thanks. / Thanks a lot.**

D 🎤 **Make it personal** In pairs, role-play. Then change roles.
A: You go to a fast-food restaurant.
B: You're the server. Take the order.

Can I help you?
A ..., please.

Writing 5 A reply on social media

*I hate you I love you,
I hate that I want you,
You want her, you need her,
And I'll never be her.*

A ▶ 5.25 Read Claudia's reply to a social media post. Check the photos of the food on her pizza. Answer 1 and 2.

1 Who doesn't like "Chickibeans Pizza"?
2 Do they all eat *churros*?

FOODCHAT   Login

Nicola J
Posted 3.56 p.m.

Hi everyone, I need ideas for a special dish for a dinner party. Any suggestions?

Share Like Comment
3 comments

Claudia C

Posted 3.56 p.m.

Hi Nicola, I have an unusual idea! My brother Carlos always wants the same thing for ¹**his / him** birthday. We call it "Chickibeans Pizza", and we ²**sometimes / always** make it for ³**his / him**, every year. It's a pizza with chicken, cheese, tomatoes, carrots and beans. It sounds horrible, but he loves ⁴**it / them**. My sister hates beans so she doesn't like it, but that's good for Carlos because he can eat more! Then we have delicious *churros* from the Portuguese store on 4th Avenue. We all love ⁵**it / them**! I can send you a great recipe for *churros* if you want to make ⁶**it / them** too?

B Reread and choose the correct word in 1–6.

C Read *Write it right!* and circle one example of each of the six rules in Claudia's reply.

> ✓ **Write it right!**
>
> Use capital letters:
> 1 for names
> 2 street names
> 3 nationalities
> Use commas (,):
> 4 after an introduction
>   *Hello Nicola, here's a dish I love.*
> 5 for items in a list
> 6 Don't use *the* to talk about food in general.
>   *I don't really like pasta.* NOT ~~I don't really like the pasta.~~

D Match questions 1–4 to answers a–d.
1 What's the name of your dish?
2 Who usually makes it, and when?
3 What are the important ingredients?
4 Who really likes it? Who doesn't like it? Why?

a ☐ There are a lot of different recipes. I use onions, garlic, olive oil, tomatoes, saffron, and a lot of seafood and fish.
b ☐ All my family love it, except my sister because she's a vegetarian.
c ☐ It's *paella*.
d ☐ My dad usually makes it on weekends.

E **Make it personal** Write a reply to Nicola's social media post.

Before	Think of a special dish, and answers to 1–4 in **D**. Use a dictionary for words you don't know in English.
While	Follow the rules in *Write it right!* Offer to send Nicola the recipe.
After	Check your reply carefully with a partner. Post it to your class.

68

5 It's about taste

1 Before watching

A Complete the dialogue with these words.

| hungry | ~~looks~~ | pay for |
| tastes | try | vegetarian |

A: Wow, that chicken sandwich ___looks___ good.
 I'm _____. Can I _____ it by credit card?
 Thanks.
 Mmm. It _____ delicious. Really great! Do you
 want to _____ it?
B: No, thanks. I'm a _____.

B Put the foods in the correct columns. Which do you eat every week?

beef	bread	breadsticks	burgers	chicken
dessert	fish	French fries	fruit	meat
pasta	rice	salad	vegetables	

Vegetarian foods	Non-vegetarian foods

I eat fruit every day, but I never eat dessert.

C 🗣 Make it personal **Schedules** In pairs, guess your partner's answers to 1 and 2.
1 How many hours a week do you work, study, and sleep?
2 When are your days off?

I work from 8:30 a.m. to 5:30 p.m., from Monday to Friday. That's 45 hours a week.

2 While watching

A Look at the photo and the chart. In pairs, try to guess Genevieve's weekly schedule. Then watch until 2:15 and check the days Genevieve does these things.

	Mo	Tu	We	Th	Fr	Sa	Su
1 work							
2 go to class							
3 go to the gym							
4 take singing lessons							
5 practice singing							
6 practice guitar							
7 a day off							
8 study							

B Watch again to check and write her work and class times. What does she want to do on Saturday mornings and evenings?

Times	Work	Class
Monday & Wednesday	9–4 & __–__	__–__ & __–__
Tuesday		__–__
Thursday	__–__ & __–__	in the afternoon

C Complete extracts 1–4 with the words.

| always | every day | four days a week |
| usually | weekends | |

1 What hours do you _____ work?
2 I practice singing and guitar _____.
3 I work _____ and _____, so I understand.
4 Are you _____ so busy?

D True (T) or false (F)?
1 Rory manages the schedule at ID Café.
2 He doesn't have a day off.
3 Genevieve likes her schedule.
4 Rory works to pay for school.
5 Genevieve and Rory like to be busy.

E Watch the complete video and (circle) the correct word or phrase.
1 Rory puts the dinner specials on the menu in the **morning / afternoon**.
2 Today's special is **Midwestern burger / Kentucky chicken** and French fries.
3 **Genevieve / Rory** doesn't eat beef.
4 Genevieve likes **everything on the menu / only the salads and sandwiches**.
5 **Rory / Genevieve** loves the desserts.
6 **The cook tries / Rory and the cook try** everything before it goes on the menu.

3 After watching

A 🗣 Make it personal Role-play a similar schedule interview. If you have a job, talk about yourself. If not, A: You're Rory. B: You're Genevieve. Then change roles.

So, what hours do you usually work?

69

Hey now, you're an all-star, get your game on, go play,
Hey now, you're a rock star, get the show on, get paid.

- A How old / your … ?
- B Name three European countries.

- A When / meet friends?
- B Give your opinion of an actor.

- A Name four personal objects you have with you.
- B What / usually do / weekends?

- A Count from 3 to 33, three by three.
- B Name four kinds of fruit or vegetables.

- A … children?
- B Name? From? Job?

- A What kind / food / like?
- B Name three male family members.

- A Say six colors.
- B What / phone number?

- A Say three alternate days of the week.
- B Give your opinion of a singer or sports celebrity.

- A Give your opinion of a book or movie.
- B How old / you?

- A … married?
- B Spell the name of your city.

- A Name four personal objects you don't have with you.
- B When / watch movies?

71

Grammar Unit 1

1A *a / an* and *the*

Dora is **a teacher**.   She's **an excellent teacher**.
ID is **a book**.   It's **an English book**.
New York is **a city**.   It's **a big city**.

Use *a / an* for a non specific person, place, or thing = "one."

Use *a* before a consonant sound:
▸ a <u>m</u>an, a <u>ch</u>air, a <u>b</u>ook.
Use *an* before a vowel sound:
▸ an <u>a</u>pple, an <u>e</u>mail, an <u>i</u>con, an <u>o</u>pera, an <u>u</u>rgent email.
Exception:
▸ a <u>u</u>niversity, a <u>u</u>niform (the *u* is pronounced with a consonant sound /ju:/)

The teacher is Dora.   Where is **the elevator**? (singular)
Welcome to **the New ID School of English**.   **The museums** in DC are fantastic. (plural)

Use *the* for:
▸ a specific noun: **the** President, **the** capital city
▸ singular or plural: **the** Natural History Museum, **the** museums.

a / an = singular = **a tablet**.

1B Verb *be* ⊕ ⊖

The verb *be* has three forms: *am, is, are*.

⊕	Contractions	⊖	Contractions
I **am** single.	I**'m** single.	I **am not** married.	I**'m not** married.
You **are** married.	You**'re** married.	You **are not** single.	You**'re not** / **aren't** single.
It **is** a problem!	It**'s** a problem!	It **is not** good.	It**'s not** / **isn't** good!

You = singular and plural
You're **a student** = one
You're **students** = two or more

Use contractions when you speak or write informal texts.
Note: Don't contract *am + not*. Remember the subject.
I'm not. NOT ~~I amn't.~~
I'm Mexican. NOT ~~Am Mexican.~~

1C Verb *be* ❓

Yes / No questions & Short answers

❓ Be + Subject	⊕ S + be	⊖ S + be + not
Are you married?	Yes, I **am**.	No, I**'m not**.
Is it a 5G phone? **Is** this your pen?	Yes, it **is**.	No, it**'s not**. / No, it **isn't**.

Invert the subject (S) and the verb (V) to form a question.
Are you Peruvian? NOT ~~You are Peruvian?~~
Yes / No questions have a short answer.
Note: Don't contract ⊕ short answers.
Are you American? Yes, I am. NOT ~~Yes, I'm.~~

Wh- questions

❓ Wh-Question + be + S	Full Answer	Short Answer
Where are you from?	I **am** / I**'m** from Brazil.	Brazil.
How are you?	I **am** / I**'m** fine, thanks.	Fine, thanks.
What's your name? **What's** this?	It **is** / It**'s** Marcos. It **is** / It**'s** a tablet.	Marcos. A tablet.

Form a *Wh-* question with *Wh-* question word + *be* + S.
Where are you from? NOT ~~From where are you?~~
Answer *Wh-* questions with information.
Contraction: **What's, Where's, How's**.
Note: Don't contract *Wh-* questions + *are*.
Where are ...? or How are ... ? NOT ~~Where're ...? How're ...?~~

Unit 1

1A

1 Circle the correct words.
1 Look at **a** / **the** photo in **a** / **the** book.
2 What's **an** / **the** eraser?
3 This is **an** / **the** apple. It's for **a** / **the** teacher.
4 "W" is **a** / **the** letter in **an** / **the** English alphabet.
5 Buenos Aires is **a** / **the** great city. It's **a** / **the** capital of Argentina.

2 Complete 1–5 with **a** / **an** where necessary.
1 This is _____ book.
2 Pedro and Mariana are _____ students.
3 Is this _____ credit card or _____ ID card?
4 I have _____ dog called Maya and _____ energetic cat called Luna.
5 Is this _____ letter "O" or _____ zero?

3 Correct the mistake in 1–5.
1 I'm student.
   I'm a student.
2 You're from U.S.
3 I'm from the Brazil.
4 This is the my friend.
5 Shhhh! Teacher is here.
6 The parking lot is in the Terminal 2.

4 Write **the** where necessary.
1 *The* book is on _____ table.
2 _____ teacher _____ is _____ in _____ classroom.
3 Look _____ at _____ photo _____ and _____ repeat _____ sentences.
4 What's _____ email _____ of _____ school?
5 This _____ is _____ President of _____ Colombia.

1B

1 Complete with **am**, **are**, or **is**.
1 ID _____ an English book.
2 I _____ from Peru. This _____ my friend from Italy.
3 You _____ a student.
4 This _____ my email address.
5 _____ this an eraser?

2 Make sentences 1–5 negative. Use contractions where possible.
1 This is a book.   _____
2 You're my friend.   _____
3 I'm from Europe.   _____
4 This is my car.   _____
5 You're my favorite teacher.   _____

1C

1 Match the questions and answers.
1 Are you single?   ☐ No, it's a tablet.
2 Is this an English   ☐ I'm from Egypt.
   class?   ☐ Yes, it is.
3 Where are you from?   ☐ No, I'm not.
4 Are you from France?   ☐ Yes, I'm from Paris.
5 Is this a computer?

2 Complete the dialogue 1–9 with the correct form of **be** (⊕ or ⊖)

Jorge Hi. I ¹_____ Jorge. Nice to meet you.
          a [_____]
Linda My name ²_____ Linda. Nice to meet you too.
Juan   Hello, Linda! ᵇ [_____]
Linda Hi, Juan. I ³_____ fine, thanks.
Juan   Cool!
Linda Juan, this ⁴_____ Jorge.
Jorge Nice to meet you. ᶜ [_____]
Juan   I ⁵_____ from Mexico. And you? ⁶_____ you from Spain?
Jorge Yes, I ⁷_____!
Juan   Cool! Hey Linda, ᵈ [_____]?
Linda It ⁸_____ my flash drive. It ⁹_____ for my documents.
Juan   Cool!

3 Now write **Wh-** questions in the boxes to complete the dialogue. Use contractions where possible.

Grammar Unit 2

2A Verb *be*

Contractions

	⊕ S + *be*	⊖ S + *be* + *not*	
Singular	I'm You're He's / She's / It's	I'm not You're not / You aren't He / She / It's not He / She / It isn't	American. 20 years old. from China.
Plural	We're You're They're	We're not / We aren't You're not / You aren't They're not / They aren't	

Use verb *be* to:
- describe people and things.
- talk about age and nationality.

To ask about age, use **How old** + verb **be**.

How old	is	he / she / it? Bill / Shakira / your car?
	are	you / we / they? Fred and George / your dogs?

Yes / No questions

	❓ *Be* + S	⊕ S + *be*	⊖ S + *be* + *not*
Singular	Is *he* / *Bill* American? Is *she* / *Shakira* a musician? Is *it* / *a spider* an insect?	Yes, *he* is. Yes, *she* is. Yes, *it* is.	No, *he's* not. / No, *he isn't*. No, *she's* not. / No, *she isn't*. No, *it's* not. / No, *it isn't*.
Plural	Are *they* / *The Killers* British?	Yes, *they* are.	No, *they're* not. / No, *they aren't*.

Wh- questions (Where ... from?)

	❓ *Wh-* Q + *be* + S		⊕ S + *be* + information	
Singular	Where	is *he* / *Bill* is *she* / *Oprah* is *it* / *your car*	from?	He's She's It's	Mexican. from Mexico.
Plural		are *they* / *the Simpsons*		They're	

Use **who** for people.
- Who's Bill Gates?

Use **what** for ideas, animals or things.
- What's your address?

The 3rd person singular has three forms: **he, she, it**.
The 3rd person plural has one form: **they**.

2B Personal pronouns

They're my brothers.

We are the champions!

Am I "he" or "she?"
It's a dog!

The seven personal pronouns in English are:
I, you, he, she, it, we, they.

Use:
- **he** for a man
- **she** for a woman
- **it** for an idea, an animal, or a thing
- **you** for singular or plural
- **we** and **they** for plural.

2C Adjectives

Elle Fanning is **an excellent actor**.
Is Ricardo **a good teacher**?
We're **happy students**.
Dua Lipa and Drake are **fantastic musicians**.

In English, **adjectives** go before **nouns**.
NOT ~~She's an actor excellent.~~
Adjectives have only one form for singular and plural, and no gender.
NOT ~~We're happys students.~~

Form:
Use noun **+s** to form plurals: *a book, two books; a pen, two pens.*
- They're good student**s**.
- I'm 30 year**s** old.

Use **a / an** before occupations (singular).
- I'm **a** student.
- He's **an** Argentinian actor.

Unit 2

2B

1 Circle the correct option.
1. Bob and I **am** / **are** students. **Are** / **We're** good friends.
2. **Are** / **Is** James Bond American?
3. I think iPads **are** / **is** incredible!
4. A **Are** / **Is** you and your teacher American?
   B My teacher **'re** / **'s** American, but I **'m** / **'s** Canadian.
5. A How old **are** / **is** Jim and Tim?
   B They **'re** / **'s** 17.

2 Insert verb *be* where appropriate. Use contractions.
1. A you a good soccer player?
   B No, I not. But I a big soccer fan!
2. Paul 25 years old, and he an excellent teacher!
3. This movie not good. It terrible!
4. A Rihanna and Ed Sheeran British?
   B No, they not. She from Barbados and he British.
5. A How old you and your friends?
   B I 22 and they 21.

3 Put 1–8 in order to make questions. Then match them to the answers.
1. old / Lucy / 18 / is / years / ?
2. Jackie / who / 's / ?
3. Japan / your / friend / is / from / ?
4. are / your / names / what / ?
5. how / is / Luis / old / ?
6. Juan / is / a / musician / ?
7. Julie / and / Celia / are / your names / ?
8. from / where / 's / Samira / ?

☐ He's 18.
☐ Yes, they are.
☐ She's from Turkey.
☐ She's my teacher.
☐ No, he isn't. He's from Portugal.
☐ Yes, he is. He's an actor too.
☐ No, she isn't.
☐ Julie and Celia.

4 Look at the ID cards. Complete 1–8 with **'s**, **is**, or **isn't**. Use contractions where possible.
1. How old _____ Mario?
2. Mario _____ 23 today. It _____ his birthday!
3. Mario _____ Mexican. He _____ Spanish. He _____ from Bilbao.
4. Celine _____ 21 years old. She _____ only 18.
5. This _____ Celine Soucy. She _____ Canadian.
6. A _____ Angela really 21?
   B Yes, she _____. Look! This is her ID card.
7. Angela _____ Brazilian. She _____ from Monterrey.
8. Celine _____ a teacher. She _____ an English student at the **ID** School of English.

2B

1 Substitute the underlined words in 1–5 with pronouns.
1. <u>Laura</u> is a teacher.
2. <u>Pedro and I</u> are from Honduras.
3. <u>Emma Watson and Daniel Craig</u> are British celebrities.
4. <u>My car</u> is Chinese.
5. <u>Mexican movies</u> are fantastic!

2 Complete 1–5 with personal pronouns.
1. A Are _____ students?
   B Yes, _____ are.
2. This is Ana. _____'s my Paraguayan friend.
3. Fred and Maria are Cuban. _____'re very similar. _____'re 25, _____'re single, and _____ like rap music.
4. A Is this an Android phone?
   B No, _____'s not. _____'s an iPhone.
5. A Where's Rosa from?
   B _____'s from Costa Rica. _____'s a beautiful place.

2C

1 Correct the mistakes in 1–5.
1. Imagine Dragons are a rock band famous.
2. This is my car new.
3. *Ad Astra* and *Avengers: Endgame* is excellents movies.
4. We not goods baseball players.
5. A This is important exercise.
   B Yes, is.

2 Order 1–5 to make sentences.
1. is / fantastic / Ben Affleck / actor / a / American
2. this / urgent / an / e-mail / is
3. excellent / games / *Zombies* and *Dishonored* / are / video
4. a / Brazilian / soccer / Neymar / is / player
5. my / is / musician / Billie Eilish / favorite

Grammar Unit 3

3A Possessive adjectives

I'm a student. This is **my** course book.
You're my friend. Give me **your** address.
He's married. **His** wife is Rosa.
She lives downtown. This is **her** house.
We work a lot. **Our** office is very busy.
They're dogs. **Their** names are Don and Bel.

The seven possessive adjectives in English are:
I → My   You → Your   He → His   She → Her   It → Its   We → Our   They → Their

3B Simple present: *I / you / we / they* ⊕ ⊖ ❓

	⊕ Subject + Infinitive	
I You We They My friends	*have* a dog. *live* in Rio de Janeiro. *work* in a bank.	
	⊖ S + Auxiliary (*do*) + *not* + I	
	do not don't	*have* a car. *live* in Berlin. *work* in a store.

Use the simple present to talk about facts and routine.
The forms for *I / You / We / They* are exactly the same in ⊕, ⊖ and ❓.
Contraction: *do not* = *don't*
Use the auxiliary verb *do* to form negatives and questions.
▸ We don't know. NOT ~~We no know~~.
▸ Do you understand? NOT ~~You understand?~~
Use *in* + city, part of a city, and buildings.
▸ I live **in** NYC, and I work **in** a school **in** Soho.
Use *at* + home:
▸ Do you work **at** home?

Yes / No questions: ASI

A	S	I	⊕ S + A		⊖ S + A + not
Do	you we they	*live* in NYC? *work*? *have* a car?	Yes,	I you we they	do.	No,	I you we they	don't.

Wh- questions: QASI

Q	A	S	I		
Where	do	you we they your parents	*live*? *work*?	I You We They	*live* downtown. *work* in a hospital.
What	do	you	do?	I	'm a doctor.

3C Simple present: *he / she / it* ⊕ ⊖ ❓

	⊕ S + I	
He Tom Your son She Berta Your sister	*has* a dog. *lives* in Quito. *works* in a hospital.	
	⊖ S + A (*do*) + *not* + I	
	does not doesn't	*have* a cat. *live* in London. *work* in a bank.

Yes / No questions: ASI

A	S	I	⊕
Does	he / Leo / your son she / Ana / your sister it / your cell phone	*live* near here? *work* at home? *have* 5G?	Yes, he / she / it **does**. ⊖ No, he / she / it **doesn't**.

Form:
⊕ Use *Does* + Subject + Infinitive

Wh- questions: QASI

	⊕ S + I	
The café It	*has* Internet access.	
	⊖ S + A (*do*) + *not* + I	
	does not doesn't	*have* a printer.

Q	A	S	I	
What	does	he / Ed / your son it / your cell phone	do? have?	He *works* in a school. It *has* a good camera.

Form:
⊕ Use *he*, *she* and *it* + infinitive + *s*.
⊖ Use *does* + *not* (= *doesn't*) + infinitive.
He doesn't study. NOT ~~He no studies~~.
Does he have a car? NOT ~~Has he a car?~~

Simple present verbs have only two forms: the infinitive and the 3rd person form (*he / she / it*).
The 3rd person = verb + *s* (see spelling rules on p.78)
Exceptions: *have* → *has*   *do* → *does*

Unit 3

3A

1 Correct the mistakes.
1 This is my sister Jane, and this is she's husband.
2 His 20 years old, and he's brother is 22.
3 Do you live with you're parents?
4 Where are Daniel and he's wife from?
5 Their my children. They're names are Diego and Alejandra.
6 We don't know he. He's not us friend.
7 She's married. She lives with your husband.

2 Circle the correct option.
1 Jack's not happy. **He's / His / Your** parents are very strict.
2 Emma's really cool! Look at **his / her / she's** new jeans!
3 Nice to meet you. Is this **he's / his / your** son?
4 My husband and I live with **your / our / their** son and **his / her / our** wife.
5 Isabel and Carlos are new to the city. **Their / They're / They** children go to the local school.

3B

1 Complete 1–4 with the verbs and *in* or *at* where necessary. Then match them to photos a–d.

have (×2)   (not) have (×2)   (not) like
live (×2)   study   work (×2)

1 I _____ a lot because I _____ a lot of exams.
  I _____ time to see my friends. It's horrible.
2 We _____ two children. They're beautiful! We _____ an apartment and I _____ home.
3 I _____ a restaurant, but I _____ my job.
4 We _____ alone and we _____ children, but we're very happy.

3C

1 Circle the correct form.
1 **Do / Does** Johnny **work / works** in Mexico City?
2 My friends **have / has** two children.
3 Celia and her sister **don't / doesn't** live alone. Their mother **live / lives** in their house too.
4 Oscar **don't / doesn't** work freelance. He **work / works** for an online company.
5 Where **do / does** he **work / works**?

2 Complete 1–5 and a–e with *do*, *don't*, *does* or *doesn't*. Then match the questions and answers.
1 _____ you have a big family?
2 _____ Mireya work downtown?
3 _____ your children study in Chicago?
4 _____ you and your husband work at home?
5 _____ Rodrigo want to be a hairdresser?
a ☐ Yes, they _____.
b ☐ No, I _____.
c ☐ Yes, he _____.
d ☐ No, she _____.
e ☐ Yes, we _____.

3 Read the answers and complete the questions.
1 A Where _____?
  B I work in a drugstore.
2 A _____ alone?
  B No, we live with our father.
3 A _____ your grandparents _____?
  B No, they don't. They're retired.
4 A What _____ your siblings _____?
  B My sister's a cashier and my brother's at college.
5 A _____ exactly?
  B We live in downtown Philadelphia. It's a great city. _____ _____ know it?

Grammar Unit 4

4A There + be

There's a charger in my bag.
There isn't a teacher in the classroom.
Is there a subway station on this street?
Use **There + be** to indicate the existence of something.
NOT ~~It's a charger in my bag.~~

Singular

+	There is / There's	an umbrella in my car. one credit card in my bag.
−	There isn't	a coin in my purse.
?	Is there	a good show on TV tonight? a cell phone in your bag? a virus on your computer?
Short Answers	+ Yes, *there is*. − No, *there isn't*.	

There are two cars in the garage.
Are there a lot of apps on your phone?

Plural

+	There are	two umbrellas in my car.
−	There aren't	a lot of students here today.
?	Are there	computers in the classroom? mints in your purse? keys in your bag?
Short Answers	+ Yes, *there are*. − No, *there aren't*.	

Contractions: *there is = there's, there is not = there isn't, there are not = there aren't*
But *there are* NOT ~~there're~~

4B this / that / these / those

		Singular	Plural
Here		What's **this**? **This** is a cell phone. **This** book is good.	What are **these**? **These** are earphones. **These** students are incredible.
There		What's **that**? **That's** your ID. **That** woman is my teacher.	What are **those**? **Those** are your keys. **Those** tablets are new.

Use *this / these* for items with you, near you, or "here".
NOT ~~What's that here?~~
Use *that / those* for items with other people, distant from you, or "there".
NOT ~~What are these there?~~

4C Plural nouns

Regular plurals

+ -s	consonant + y = - y + -ies	s, sh, ch, x + -es
a pen – pens	a dictionary – dictionaries	a class – classes
a book – books	a country – countries	a toothbrush – toothbrushes
an actor – actors	a nationality – nationalities	a beach – beaches
a cell phone – cell phones	a city – cities	a church – churches
a key – keys	a celebrity – celebrities	a box – boxes
a photo – photos	a baby – babies	a bus – buses
a month – months	an activity – activities	Pronounce *-es* as an extra syllable: /ɪz/
a year – years		
a comb – combs		

The plural of most nouns = noun + s

Irregular plurals

Different forms
a man – **men**
a woman – **women**
a child – **children**
a person – **people**
a wife – **wives**

Unit 4

4A

1 Order the words to make sentences.
1 twenty / are / there / students / in / class / our
2 police officers / are / there / in / New York City / excellent
3 charger / is / on the table / there / white / a
4 rulers / on / the desk / are / there / two
5 there / a / ring / 's / box / in the

2 Complete 1–5 with 's, is, isn't, are or aren't.
1 There _____ a black camera here. _____ it your camera?
2 There _____ a lot of students in this class. There _____ only one.
3 _____ there a lot of people in your family?
4 A _____ there a new photo of you on Facebook?
   B Yes, there _____! It's me and my mom.
5 All the restaurants in my city are expensive! There _____ one cheap restaurant!

4B

1 Complete 1–5 with this, these, that or those.

1 What are _____? Candies? No, they're pens!

2 _____ watches are beautiful!

3 Is _____ a cell phone? No, it's a mini tablet.

4 _____ red apple is delicious!

5 _____'s a really good movie!

4C

1 Change sentences 1–5 to the plural.
1 What's that? Your new diary? _____
2 This is a slow bus! _____
3 That's a beautiful fish. _____
4 Is this your blue toothbrush? _____
5 This isn't a camera, it's a cell phone. _____

Grammar Unit 5

5A like / love / don't like / hate

really hate — hate — don't like — like — really like — love

Use these verbs to talk about how we feel about things.
Use plural forms with countable nouns.
- I **hate** apples. **NOT** I hate apple.
- She really **likes** eggs.

Don't use **the** + nouns to talk about things in general.
- He **doesn't like** chicken. **NOT** He doesn't like the chicken.
- We **love** oranges. **NOT** We love the oranges.
- My dad doesn't like soccer.
- I hate Mondays!

5B Frequency adverbs

Frequency	What do people do on Sundays?
100% ↑ ↓ 0%	I **always** go to church. We **usually** watch a movie. My brother **sometimes** goes to the gym. Donna **never** stays home.

Use these adverbs to say how frequently things occur.
Frequency adverbs usually go:
- before **main verbs**: I **always watch** soccer on Sundays.
- after verb **be** and **auxiliaries**: She **is never** late. She **doesn't usually** study for exams.

Prepositions:
Use **in** + the with parts of the day.
- I always eat fruit **in** the mornings.
- Do you watch TV **in** the evenings?

Use **at** + times and night.
- My dad works at night. He starts at 10 p.m. and finishes at 6 a.m.

Use **on** with the weekend, days, or days + parts of the day.
- My mother works **on** the weekend.
- I never eat meat **on** Fridays.
- We study English **on** Thursday evenings.

5C Possessive 's & object pronouns

Possessive 's
Use **'s** to indicate possession.
The **teacher's** phone. (singular, one teacher, one phone)
The **teachers'** phones. (plural, two teachers, plural phones)
The **children's** phones. (irregular plural)
Beyoncé**'s** music. **NOT** The music of Beyoncé.

Subject	Object	
I	me	I love you. Do you love **me**?
You	you	You're a terrible person. I don't like **you**.
He	him	Bruce Springsteen is OK. I like **him**.
She	her	What do you think of Pink? Do you like **her**?
It	it	Japanese food is OK, but I don't often eat **it**.
We	us	We're here. Please, listen to **us**!
They	them	My parents are great. I live with **them**. There are good movies on TV, but I never watch **them**.

Use **object pronouns**:
- to substitute people and things when they are the object of a sentence.
- usually **after** a verb or preposition.

Do you use social media? Yes, I use **it** a lot. **NOT** I use a lot.
Do you like Shawn Mendes? Yes, I love **him**! **NOT** I love!

Unit 5

5A

1 Correct the mistakes.
1. Mark don't like a Chinese food.
2. My children don't eat vegetables for the lunch.
3. Does your mother drinks coffee for the breakfast?
4. I not like meat very much, but my brother do.
5. What kind of fruit do your daughter likes?
6. Do your childs like the soccer?

2 Use the prompts to write sentences / questions.
1. I / hate / carrots
2. My sister / not like / cheese
3. you / like / swimming ?
4. I / really like / Italian / food
5. your son / like / black coffee ?
6. I / love / fish / but / my brother / not like / it / very much
7. you / eat / a lot of / meat ?

5B

1 Look at Gina's schedule. Complete a–e with *in* or *on*. Then match 1–5 to a–e.
1. Gina sometimes goes to the gym
2. She always goes to the grocery store
3. She always goes to church
4. She never watches TV
5. She usually works

a ☐ _____ Saturday mornings.
b ☐ _____ the weekends.
c ☐ _____ the afternoons.
d ☐ _____ Sunday afternoons.
e ☐ _____ Sunday mornings.

	Sunday	Monday	Tuesday	Wednesday	Thursday	Friday	Saturday
9:00 12:00							
13:00 18:00							
18:00 22:00							

2 Order the words to make sentences.
1. the / they / cook / food / special / weekends / on / always
2. never / we / go / on / to / school / Sundays
3. watch / in / always / TV / evenings / the / I / don't
4. the / do / you / go / to / movies / on / weekends / the ?
5. Chinese / at / they / eat / never / food / home
6. on / often / mornings / play / Sunday / soccer / Scott / doesn't
7. the gym / go / sometimes / to / Saturdays / the / I / on
8. every / they / class / day / a / take / do?

5C

1 Correct the mistakes in the answers in 1–5.
1. A Do you like Taylor Swift?
   B No, I don't like she. She's music is terrible.
2. A Do your children like Disney movies?
   B Yes, they love. They watch it every day.
3. A What do you think about Ryan Reynolds?
   B He's a good actor. I like he!
4. A Do you like the *Avengers* movies?
   B We don't like it. We hate superhero movies.
5. A What do you think about Thai food?
   B I really like them. Let's go to a Thai restaurant now.
6. A Does your boyfriend like Selena Gómez?
   B Yes, he loves. Personally, I don't like she!

2 Complete 1–5 with *him*, *her*, *it*, or *them*. Then (circle) five possessive *'s* in the conclusion.
1. Mary loves her boyfriend, but he doesn't love _____.
2. Her brother's very intelligent, but she never listens to _____.
3. Mary likes apples a lot, but she never eats _____.
4. She really likes coffee. She drinks _____ a lot.
5. Her dogs are terrible. We don't like _____.

Conclusion
Mary's boyfriend's not in love with her. Mary's brother's very intelligent, but she ignores this. Mary's favorite fruit is apple, and coffee's Mary's favorite drink. Finally, Mary's dogs aren't very nice.

Sounds and usual spellings

S Difficult sounds for Spanish speakers
P Difficult sounds for Portuguese speakers

▶ To listen to these words and sounds, and to practice them, go to the pronunciation section on the Richmond Learning Platform.

Vowels

/iː/	three, tree, eat, receive, believe, key, B, C, D, E, G, P, T, V, Z
/ɪ/	six, mix, it, fifty, fish, trip, lip, fix
/ʊ/	book, cook, put, could, cook, woman
/uː/	two, shoe, food, new, soup, true, suit, Q, U, W
/ɛ/	pen, ten, heavy, then, again, men, F, L, M, N, S, X
/ə/	bananas, pajamas, family, photography

/ɜr/	shirt, skirt, work, turn, learn, verb
/ɔr/	four, door, north, fourth
/ɔ/	walk, saw, water, talk, author, law
/æ/	man, fan, bad, apple
/ʌ/	sun, run, cut, umbrella, country, love
/ɑ/	hot, not, on, clock, fall, tall
/ɑr/	car, star, far, start, party, artist, R

Diphthongs

/eɪ/	plane, train, made, stay, they, A, H, J, K
/aɪ/	nine, wine, night, my, pie, buy, eyes, I, Y
/aʊ/	house, mouse, town, cloud

| /ɔɪ/ | toys, boys, oil, coin |
| /oʊ/ | nose, rose, home, know, toe, road, O |

□ Voiced
□ Unvoiced

Sounds and usual spellings

Consonants

/p/	pig, pie, open, top, apple
/b/	bike, bird, describe, able, club, rabbit
/m/	medal, monster, name, summer
/w/	web, watch, where, square, one
/f/	fish, feet, off, phone, enough
/v/	vet, van, five, have, video
/θ/	teeth, thief, thank, nothing, mouth
/ð/	mother, father, the, other
/t/	truck, taxi, hot, stop, attractive
/d/	dog, dress, made, adore, sad, middle
/n/	net, nurse, tennis, one, sign, know
/l/	lion, lips, long, all, old

/s/	snake, skate, kiss, city, science
/z/	zoo, zebra, size, jazz, lose
/ʃ/	shark, shorts, action, special, session, chef
/ʒ/	television, treasure, usual
/k/	cat, cake, back, quick
/g/	goal, girl, leg, guess, exist
/ŋ/	king, ring, single, bank
/h/	hand, hat, unhappy, who
/tʃ/	chair, cheese, kitchen, future, question
/dʒ/	jeans, jump, generous, bridge
/r/	red, rock, ride, married, write
/j/	yellow, yacht, university

83

Audioscript

Unit 1

◐ 1.15 Notice th = /ð/ or /θ/. Notice /eu/ and /iː/.

D = Doctor   M = Mr. Jones
D Now, Mr. Jones, please read the letters and numbers in line one.
M A-H-J-K-8.
D OK. Line two?
M B-C-D-E-G...
D And then?
M P-T-V-Z-3.
D And line three?
M Uh ... F-L ... M-N ... uh ... S-X ... 7?
D Good and line four?
M Uh ... I-Y-5-9 ...
D Good, and the final line?
M O? No, no. Q. Q-U-W. And, uh ... R? No, no, 2? I don't know!
D That's OK. Thank you!

◐ 1.18 Notice /ae/ and /j/.

Part 1
D = Daniel   A = Angela
D Hi Angela!
A Hi! ... Hmmm, Sorry ... Oh ... are you in my English class?
D At the New ID School of English? Yes, I am. My name's Daniel.
A Ah, yes, of course. I recognize you. How are you?
D I'm fine, thanks. How are you?
A I'm fine, too. Please, sit down.
D Thanks. Coffee?
A Yes. Yes, please. Thank you.

Part 2
A ... good idea. Let's meet and study together.
D OK! What's your phone number?
A It's 78190366.
D And, what's your name? Angela ...?
A Ochoa. Angela Ochoa.
D Can you spell that, please?
A O-C-H-O-A. It's a Mexican name.
D Oh, are you on WhatsApp?
A Yes, I am. Message me.
D OK. Yes. So ....see you soon!
A Yes and thanks for the coffee. Bye.

◐ 1.23 Notice spelling of final /m/ and the intonation in the questions.

R = Receptionist   A = Antonio
R Next!
A Good morning. How are you? ↘
R Fine, thanks. What's your name, please? ↘
A Chaves. Antonio Chaves.
R Is that C-H-A-V-E-Z? ↗
A No, C-H-A-V-E-S.
R Oh, are you from Caracas? ↗
A No, I'm from Rio de Janeiro.
R What's your email address, please? ↘
A It's toni.ch@gvr.com.
R Can you repeat that, please? ↗
A Sure! Toni—that's T-O-N-I, dot C-H, at G-V-R dot com.
R Thanks. And what's your phone number? ↘
A 21 8977 4053.
R Thank you. OK, here's your student ID card.
A Thanks. Bye.
R Goodbye.

◐ 1.26 Notice /u/, /uː/, and final /d/.

1 A Hello! It's so good to see you!
  B Oh, hi ...
2 A Good evening. A table for two?
  B Yes, please.
3 A OK, I'm off. Good night, everyone.
  B Bye!
  C Good night!

Unit 2

◐ 2.5 Notice /ɜr/ and s = /z/.

And this is apartment fourteen.
Nineteen kilos. Wow!
Only here: on channel seventeen ...
Thirteen liters.
Twenty dollars, please.
Fifteen miles per hour.
You're eighteen! Happy birthday!
Sixteen kilometers is ten miles.

◐ 2.6 Notice the pronunciation and spelling of /n/ and /ng/.

A = Anna   B = Ben
A OK, I read the headlines, and you guess the photos. OK?
B Sure!
A Drake Song is Big Hit.
B The ... song? Oh, of course ... Photo 6?
A Yeah! Uh ... Fans View Luis Fonsi's Pop Video 6 Billion Times!
B That's photo 7!
A Yes! Good! 100% Electric Car is Incredible Success.
B Photo 4.
A Yep. Multi-million Dollar Contract for Soccer Player.
B It's photo 3, obviously.
A Uh-huh. But who is he?
B He's Kylian Mbappé!
A Ah yes. I think he's from Madrid - or Barcelona?
B No! He isn't Spanish. He's from Paris. He's French.
A Oops! OK, next: New Movie of Famous Comic book.
B Ah, that's easy! It's Avenger's: EndGame. Photo 1.
A Wooh, yes! Oscar for Best Female Actor.
B Photo 5?
A No! She's Taylor Swift. She's a musician, not an actor.
B Of course! It's photo 2. I love Emma Stone. The movie is fantastic.
A Hmm, it isn't bad. And the next headline: Musician Posts Political Comments on Instagram.
B OK, that's Taylor Swift. Photo 5.
A Right! You're a genius!
B Hmpf!

◐ 2.8 Notice the pronunciation of t and th.

A = Anna   B = Ben
A Look! Drake's song is a big hit.
B Yes! I think it's a fantastic song! And the video is incredible.
A Mm, I agree. Is he your favorite musician?
B I think he's good, but my favorite musician is Taylor Swift. I love her!
A And who's your favorite actor?
B Emma Stone, 100 per cent.
A Yeah, I think she's a good actor too!
B OK, and what's your favorite movie?
A Uh... that's difficult. I don't know ... Avengers: End Game, I think.
B NO!!! I think it's a terrible movie! Three hourszzzzzzzzzz!

◐ 2.13 Notice unvoiced /θ/ and the connections.

A W This car's twenty-three years_old and_it's horrible!
   M How old is_it? Twenty-three? Wow, that's_ old. Very, very old!
B W How old are_you today?
   M I'm thirty-eight.
   W Happy birthday!
C W How old is_she?
   M She's forty-nine!
D M Look_at that chair. It's_an antique. How old is_it?
   M It's_about ninety-five years old, I think. And it's beautiful!

◐ 2.21 Notice voiced /ð/, /ɪ/, and /iː/.

W Look. It's Ryan Gosling; he's a fantastic actor.
M Where's he from?
W I think he's from the U.S.
M Are you sure?
W Hmmm. No, he's Canadian!
M What city is he from?
W He's from London. There's a London in Canada too! It's in Ontario.
M Really?! And how old is he?
W He's around 38.
M Is he married?
W Yes, he is ... I think. And his wife, or his girlfriend, is an actor, too.
M And who are the girls?
W They're Girls Generation. They're a K Pop band.
M K Pop? Where are they from?
W They're from Seoul in South Korea, of course!
M How old are they?
W I don't know. No idea!
M Are they married?
W Hmmm, no. I don't think they are.
M And who's she?
W I'm not sure, but she's, uh, familiar...
M Hmmm, wait. I know! She's a tennis player!
W You're right! She's Simona Halep.
M Halep? Where's she from?
W She's Romanian. She's from Constanta in Romania, and she's around 30. And I think she's married.

◐ 2.23 Notice the intonation in the questions.

1 M Where's he from? ↘
  W I think he's from the U.S.
2 M Are you sure? ↗
  W Hmm. No, he's Canadian!
3 M How old is he? ↘
  W He's around 38.
4 M Is he married? ↗
  W Yes, he is.
5 M How old are they? ↘
  W I don't know. No idea.
6 M She's a tennis player.
  W You're right. Number one in the world.

Audioscript

Review 1

▶ R1.4 Notice dark /l/ vs. normal /l/.
R = receptionist P = Pablo
R Next!
P Good morning.
R Hello. What's your name, please?
P I'm Pablo Castillo.
R Please spell your name.
P OK. It's C-A-S-T-I-L-L-O.
R Where are you from, Mr. Castillo?
P I'm Chilean, from Valparaíso.
R Are you married?
P Yes, I am.
R How old are you, please?
P I'm 36.
R OK, thank you. And what's your phone number, please?
P 312-8977-0346.
R And your email address?
P It's pabloc@qhy.net.
R Thank you.

Unit 3

▶ 3.1 Notice a = /æ/ or /ɑ/.
Don't miss FANTASTIC FAMILIES! Tonight, the topics are TV series characters and their jobs. What does your favorite TV character do? Is he or she a bank cashier, a doctor, an engineer, a police officer, a university professor? Watch Fantastic Families this evening at eight o'clock on KYZ TV.

▶ 3.2 Notice the rhyming words.
H = Host   T = Tessa   P = Paul   G = Gloria
F = Fred   M = Maria   R = Roger   S = Sophia
J = James
H Good evening, ladies and gentlemen, and welcome to Fantastic Families. I am Louie Green. And here are tonight's Fantastic Families – the Smiths and the Andersons. Hello, everyone, how are you tonight?
All Good evening. / Hi. / Fine. / Great.
H Here's team A, The Smiths. What are your names, and what do you do?
T My name's Tessa. I'm a hairdresser.
H Hah! Brilliant! Tessa, the hairdresser!
P I'm Paul and I'm a sales clerk. And this is my wife, Gloria.
G Yes, that's right! And I'm a lawyer.
H What? Gloria, the lawyer?
F Hello, everybody. I'm Fred. I'm a server.
H Thank you! What about Fantastic Families team B, The Andersons? What are your names, and what do you do?
M I'm Maria. I'm an engineer.
H Maria, the engineer!
M And this is my husband …
R Thank you, Maria, dear. My name's Roger, and I'm a police officer.
S I'm a bank cashier. My name's Sophia.
H No way! Sophia, the cashier too?
J I'm James, and I'm very happy to be here.
H Great, James! And what do you do?
J Oh, sorry! I'm an IT professional.
H Thank you all! And now let's start our quiz with the first question …

▶ 3.3 Notice the /ə/.
1
Ladies and gentlemen of the jury. This is impossible.
Answer   She's a lawyer.
2
OK, that's one hundred, two hundred, three hundred and fifty-five dollars. Thank you. Have a nice day!
Answer   She's a bank cashier.
3
OK, here you are. One coffee, one tea and a mineral water with lemon.
Answer   He's a server.
4
A OK, say "Ah!"
B Aaaagh.
A Good, good, Thanks. OK, Relax. You're OK. No problem there.
Answer   She's a doctor.
5
OK, just a little more here and a little more and … There! Beautiful!
Answer   He's a hairdresser.
6
A Uh, this shirt? It's one hundred dollars. It's beautiful, isn't it?
B Yes, I like it. Do you have it in black?
A Yes, we do. One moment. Here you are.
Answer   She's a sales clerk.
7
OK, OK. Good morning, everybody. The topic for today is "the history of feminism".
Answer   She's a university professor.
8
Yes, yes, yes! It works. This new program works! I'm rich!
Answer   He's an IT professional.
9
Stop! Hey, you! Stop right there! Stop that man! Stop! Got you. Right, you are coming with me!
Answer   She's a police officer.

▶ 3.4 Notice the sentence stress and reductions.
H = Host   P = Paul
H OK, the next topic is television. Here's question one. Ready? In the famous NBC sitcom, Friends, do you remember Friends? In Friends, what does Ross Geller do? Is he: a) a university professor, b) an actor or c) a lawyer? Yes! Paul?
P He's a university professor. Letter a.
H That's absolutely correct! David Schwimmer plays Ross Geller, a university professor at New York University. Question two is about the USA Network series Suits. Ready? What do Jessica Pearson, Harvey Specter and Louis Litt do in Suits? Are they: a) IT professionals, b) doctors or c) lawyers? Yes! Sophia?
S b! They're doctors!
H No, they aren't! Yes, Tessa?
T They're lawyers, obviously! Letter c!
H Yes, they are, Tessa! The characters are lawyers. The next question is about …

▶ 3.9 Notice the intonation in questions.
1 W2 Do you have children? ↗
   W3 Yes, I do. I have a son.
   W2 What's his name? ↘
   W3 His name's Daniel.
2 M Do you live alone? ↗
   W No, I don't. I live with my grandmother.
   M2 What's her name? ↘
   W4 Her name's Elizabeth.
3 M Do you have a big family? ↗
   W4 No. I don't have siblings. I'm an only child.

▶ 3.12 Notice the connections.
A lot of people don't have a job. But on today's program we talk to people who have not one, but two jobs. Where do they work? In a school and in a restaurant? In a hospital and a drugstore? Or in a travel agency and in a bank or an office? Do they work downtown? Do they work at home? Let's listen to their stories.

▶ 3.13 Notice /ɜr/ and the spelling of /w/ at the beginning of words.
W What do you do, Hanna?
W2 I have two jobs. I'm a personal assistant and a sales clerk.
W A personal assistant? Do you work in an office?
W2 Yes, I do. I work in a lawyer's office. But only in the mornings.
W And where do you work as a sales clerk?
W2 I work in a drugstore—I work there in the afternoons.
W Which do you prefer?
W2 Oh, personal assistant. It's very interesting.
W And what do you do, Victor?
M I'm a web designer. And I'm a server too.
W I see. Where do you work as a web designer?
M Well, I'm freelance, and I work at home. It's very convenient!
W And a server? Do you work in a bar?
M No, not a bar. I work in an Italian restaurant. It's a difficult job with a lot of stress.

▶ 3.14 Notice the connections.
W2 I work in a drugstore.
W2 Do you work in an office?
M I work at home.
M I work in a restaurant.

▶ 3.17 Notice /ð/ and the intonation at the end of the sentences and questions.
W Where are you from, Natesh? ↘
M I'm from Islamabad, Pakistan. ↘
W And you live here in New York City, right? ↗
M Yes, that's right. I live in Queens. ↘
W Do you live alone? ↗
M No, no. I live with my parents and my brother, Arul. ↘
W What do your parents do? ↘
M My parents don't work. They're retired. ↘
W And your brother? ↗ What does your brother do? ↘
M My brother doesn't have a job. ↘ He's … uhm … unemployed. ↘
W Oh. OK. Are you married, Natesh? ↗
M No, I'm not, but I have a girlfriend. Her name's Reva. ↘ She's from India. ↘
W I see … You're a limo driver, ↘ right? ↗ Where do you work? ↘
M I work in the Manhattan area, thirteen hours a day. ↘
W That's a lot, isn't it? ↗ And what do you think of your job? ↘
M Oh, I think it's very interesting! I love my limo! ↘

85

◉ 3.22 Notice the sentence stress and weak forms.

W Fantastic party!
M Yes, it is ...
W Hi. My name's **Laura**.
M Oh, hello. I'm **Charlie**. Charlie **Brown**. Yes, really. Charlie Brown. Nice to **meet** you Laura.
W Nice to meet you **too**, Charlie. Do you **live** near here?
M No. I live **downtown**. **What** about **you**?
W I live near here.
M And **what** do **you** do, **Laura**?
W I don't work at the moment. I'm unemployed, but I'm a **university student**.
M I see. **What** do you **study**?
W I study **Information Technology**—IT.
M Oh, that's interesting. I'm an **IT professional**!
W Really? That's a co**incidence**! **Where** do you **work**?
M I work for a **bank**.
W Cool! **Are** you **married**, **Charlie**?
M No, I ...
W Do you **live alone**? Do you have a **girlfriend**?
M ... I **live** with my **partner**.
W Oh, I see ... Well, OK. Great talking to you. Bye!
M Bye ...

Unit 4

◉ 4.1 Notice /ɑ/ and /ə/.

W1 Vero, what's in that purse?
W2 Oh, you know. E**very**thing! Hmm ... there's my w**a**llet, obvi**ou**sly! There **are a** l**o**t **of** c**oi**ns ...
W1 Coins? Why?
W2 Oh, I c**o**llect them - you know - coins fr**o**m diff**e**rent c**ou**ntries!
W1 Er, OK ...!
W2 Yeah, and there **are** always mints in my bag, oh, and my pills. And there's **a**n **u**mbrella – it rains **a** l**o**t here! My lipstick, **a** comb, and **a** ch**a**rger too ... Oh wait, where's my cell phone?
W1 Is this your cell phone?
W2 Yes! Thank you!

◉ 4.7 Notice final /k/, /t/, and /d/.

W Look!
M Where?
W There. On the red seat. What's that?
M Uh ... it's a bag.
W Oh no!
M Yes. Open it!
W No! You open it.
M Why?
W To find a name – an ID card?
M OK. Uh, let's see. Hmm ... What's this?

◉ 4.8 Notice the spelling of the /ɪ/ and /i:/ sounds.

M OK. Uh, let's see. Hmm ... What's this?
W Let me see. Oh, they're glasses.
M Obviously! What else ... keys ... and a cell phone. And what are these? Are they pills?
W No, they're candies.
M Huh, OK. Look, what are those?
W Let me see. They're head phones.
M Ah, of course. Bluetooth headphones. Cool.
W Is there a wallet in the bag?
M No, no wallet, ... but look here ... what's this?
W Yeah! It's an ID card!
M Hm-mm and it has a name on it. And a photo. Linda Sánchez. Great!

◉ 4.15 Notice /f/, /v/, and th.

1 W Excuse me, what time is it, please?
  M It's seven forty-five.
2 M What time is your English class?
  W It's at four thirty every day.
3 W What time does the movie start?
  M It starts at eight ten.
4 M What time is lunch?
  W It's at two o'clock.
5 W What time is your flight?
  M It's at eleven fifty.
6 M What time is it in Tokyo right now?
  W Wow! It's very early. It's five fifteen in the morning.

◉ 4.19 Notice /b/ and /p/.

W Hey, is that a new tablet?
M Yes, it is. Do you like it?
W Wow! It's beautiful!
M It has 5G Internet access.
W Cool. How many apps does it have?
M Oh, I don't know. A lot! But there's an app for emails, one for Facebook, another one for Twitter ...
W Oh, no ...! So you're online all the time!
M Is that a problem?
W Yes! It's probably impossible to talk to you now!

◉ 4.20 Notice the sentence stress and reductions.

A = Lost property Assistant   T = Tourist

T Excuse me. Is this **Lost** and **Found**?
A Yes, it is. Can I **help** you?
T Ah, good. Yes. I **lost** my **wallet**.
A OK. Do you know **where**?
T Here. In the **airport**.
A **When**? Today?
T Yes. **Today**.
A **Yes**terday?
T No! **Today**!
A Sorry! OK, and what **color** is the **wallet**?
T It's **green**.
A And is it **big** or **small**?
T It's **very** big. My **passport** and credit **cards** are in it. Oh, and around **500 dollars** too. **All** the **money** for my va**cation**!
A Oh no. I'm **sorry**. Now, let's **see** what there is in the **system**.

Review 2

◉ R2.2 Notice final /n/ and spellings of /m/.

And here is Helen Rivers with today's edition of *Common People, Uncommon Lives*. Today, Helen interviews Rosa Costa, not a celebrity, but another common person with an uncommon life. Ms. Costa is a Brazilian diplomat living in Bogotá, Colombia, for the past three years. Over to you, Helen!

◉ R2.3 Notice /h/ and /r/.

H = Helen   R = Rosa

H Thank you, Johnny. I'm Helen Rivers and I'm here in Bogotá with Rosa Costa. Hello, Rosa.
R Hello, Helen. Nice to talk to you.
H So you're a Brazilian diplomat, right?
R That's right.
H Where are you from in Brazil?
R I'm from Rio de Janeiro.
H How old are you, Antonio?
R I'm 43.
H Are you married?
R Yes, I am. My husband's name's Antonio.
H Is Antonio from Rio too?
R No, he's from Montevideo, Uruguay.
H What does he do? Is he a diplomat too?
R No, Antonio's an English teacher.
H Really? Where does he work?
R In a big school downtown.
H Do you have children?
R Yes, we have a son. His name's Marcel.
H How old is he?
R He's four years old.
H Where do you live here in Bogotá?
R We live in Chicó, a very nice part of the city.
H What do you think of Bogotá and Colombia?
R Oh, I think Colombia is a beautiful country, and Bogotá is an excellent city to live in.
H What's your favorite thing about Colombia?
R My favorite thing? Hmmm. I think it's the fruit!
H The fruit?!
R Yes. And my favorite Colombian fruit is lulo. It's delicious!

Unit 5

◉ 5.5 Notice the spelling of /i:/ and /ɛ/ sounds.

M Breakfast is my favorite meal. I eat a lot. Usually bread, cheese, eggs and orange juice. What about you?
W I just drink tea with milk.
M Really? No food? No protein?
W Well, I eat a lot of beans at lunch.
M No meat?
W No, meat is not good for you.
M Oh.
W What?
M Nothing.
W What?
M Well ...
W What?
M Soft drinks are very bad for you too, but you drink a lot of soft drinks, don't you?
W Hmmm. Well, I guess nobody is perfect.

◉ 5.7 Notice the **silent letters** and /dʒ/ sound.

W Do you eat a lot of meat, Jack?
M No, I don't.
W What about vegetables?
M I eat a lot of vegetables, and fruit too.
W Do you drink a lot of coffee?
M No, but I drink a lot of fruit juice.
W Do you eat bread?
M Yes. Usually at breakfast, with cheese. I love it!

◉ 5.9 Notice the **sentence stress** and reductions.

R = Reporter

R Richard, what kind of **food** do **you** and your friends **like**?
M1 Well, my **partner** and I like **variety**. We think **food** from **different countries** is great!
R What **kind**? Do you like **Peruvian food**, for example?
M1 Yes, very much! And we love **Italian food**, **Chinese**, **Japanese** ... In fact, we like **all food**!
R Great, thanks. And **what** about **you**, Julia?
W1 I don't like **vegetables**, but I eat them because they're good for me. My **daughter loves** them!

Audioscript

R What **kind** of **vegetables** does she **like**? Does she like **toma**toes?
W1 Yes, she does. **Tomatoes**, po**ta**toes, **ca**rrots, **let**tuce ... She's only eight, but I think she's a vege**tar**ian.
R Michael, **what** kind of **food** do you like?
M2 There's a **problem** in our **house**. My **wife** loves **meat**, but I **hate** it!
R **Does** she like all **kinds** of **meat**?
M2 She likes **beef** and **chi**cken ... Hmm ... And **fish** ... Yuck! But it's OK because we're **really** in **love**!
R **Good luck**! Now Jane, what about **you**? What kind of **food** do you like?
W2 I'm **terrible**, I really like **fast food**. I think it's **delicious**!
R Really? What's your **favorite**?
W2 All of it! I like **pizza**, **hot dogs** ... And **French fries**! Oh, **French fries**!
R Ha ha! Eat some **vegetables** too! And Tony, **what** about **you** and **your family**?
M3 We eat a lot of **fruit** at home. Except for my **father** – he really **hates fruit**!
R And what kind of **fruit** do you like?
M3 Me? Uh ... I don't know ... Uh ... **Grapes**, ba**na**nas, **oranges** ... It's just fruit.

◯ 5.11 Notice *o* and *u* = /ʌ/ and *ue* = /u:/.

Monday, no fun day.
Tuesday, blues day.
Wednesday, a little gray.
Thursday, good day.
Friday, hurray!
Saturday, we play!
Sunday, we relax all day!

◯ 5.16 Notice *s* = /s/ or /z/ and the intonation in the questions.

W Look! A collection of Ryan Gosling's movies are on boxset this weekend.
M Really? ↗ That's great! I like him a lot. He's a great actor. I think his movies are excellent.
W Hmmm. I don't like them much.
M What?! They're fantastic! And what's on TV? ↘
W Do you like Stephen Colbert's show? ↗
M Yes, I do. I really like it. Why? ↘
W Well, Michelle Obama is on his show tonight.
M Michelle Obama? ↗ Again? ↗ I think Colbert loves her!
W Well, the show is about Michelle's new book.
M Her autobiography? ↗ Oh, maybe I can read it.

◯ 5.23 Notice the **silent letters** and the spelling of /ɛ/ and /i:/.

S = server   C = customer
1 S   Can I help you?
  C1 A cheeseburger, please.
  S   Fries?
  C1 No, thanks.
  S   Anything to drink?
  C1 Yes, a cola.
  S   Large, medium or small?
  C1 Large.
  S   With ice?
  C1 No, thanks.
  S   Anything else?
  C1 No, thanks.
  S   For here or to go?
  C1 For here.
  S   That's $5.99.
  C1 There you are. Thanks.
2 S   Can I help you?
  C2 A hot dog and French fries, please.
  S   Anything to drink?
  C2 Yes. A small coffee.
  S   Cream and sugar?
  C2 Just sugar, please.
  S   Anything else?
  C2 No, thanks.
  S   For here or to go?
  C2 To go.

87

1.1 What's your name?

1 Complete the dialogue with these words.

call me   I'm   My name is   Nice to meet you

Receptionist Welcome to the New ID School of English. _____ Pablo. Nice to meet you.
Student Hello! _____ Francesca Lima. _____ too, Pablo. Please, _____ Fran.
Receptionist Hi, Fran.

2 Complete the card for the student in **1**.

ID School of English

Name: _____
Address: _35 Calle San Juan, San Jose, Costa Rica_
Phone number: _(00 506) 555 00612_

3 🧑 Make it personal Complete the card for *you*.

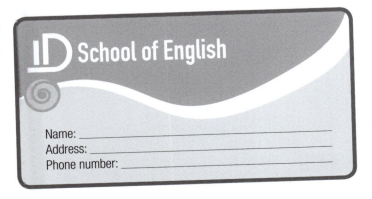

ID School of English

Name: _____
Address: _____
Phone number: _____

4 Match the words and pictures a–d.

 /i:/   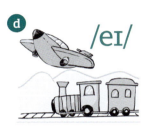 /eɪ/

☐ plane, train   ☐ two, shoe
☐ nine, wine   ☐ three, tree

5 ◯1.1 Match the groups to pictures a–d in **4**. Listen to check and repeat the words.

☐ me, meet, please, teacher
☐ name, eight, nickname, pronunciation
☐ hi, my, bye bye, five
☐ you, too, student, school

📶 Connect

Think of one extra word for categories a–d. Record them on your phone and send them to a friend or your teacher.

6 Write the numbers.

a 1   f 6
b 10   g 12
c 7   h 2
d 9   i 11
e 4   j 5

7 Complete the number puzzles.

a one, three, five, _____, _____, eleven

b three, six, nine, _____

c two, four, six, _____, _____, twelve

d eleven, nine, seven, _____, _____

e ten, nine, eight, _____, _____, five

1.2 Where are you from?

1 Match photos a–e to the classroom instructions and circle the correct verb.

- (Read) / Listen to the text.
- Look at / Complete the photo.
- Repeat / Complete the exercise.
- Read / Repeat the sentence.
- Listen to / Repeat the dialogue.

2 ▶1.2 Correct the mistake in each of instructions a–c. Listen to check.

a Please read the text and listen the CD.

c Look to the picture and complete the dialogue.

b Now look the picture and match the columns.

3 ▶1.3 Look at the photo of Javier, Alberto, and Anna. Order the dialogue, a–h. Listen to check.

- [a] Hi, Anna!
- [ ] Sure! Where are you from, Beto?
- [ ] Nice to meet you, Alberto.
- [ ] Hi, Beto. How are you? This is my friend Javier. Javier, this is Alberto.
- [ ] I'm from Brazil. And you?
- [ ] Nice to meet you too, Javier. Please, call me Beto.
- [ ] I'm from Argentina.
- [h] Oh, no! Please don't speak about soccer!

4 **Make it personal** Write questions with the verb *be* and answer them.

a What / your / name _____?
_____

b Where / you / from _____?
_____

c What / your / address _____?
_____

d What / your / telephone number _____?
_____

🔊 **Connect**

Record your answers to 4 and send them to your teacher or a friend.

1.3 What's this in English?

1 Circle the correct article in a–j.
   a It's **a** / **an** chair.
   b It's **a** / **an** online dictionary.
   c This is **a** / **an** interactive whiteboard.
   d This is **a** / **an** notebook
   e It's **a** / **an** ID card.
   f It's **a** / **an** marker.
   g This is **a** / **an** flash drive.
   h It's **a** / **an** tablet.
   i It's **a** / **an** desk.
   j And this is **a** / **an** alien!

2 Match six of the sentences in **1** to photos 1–6.

3 Complete a–h with *'m, are, 's* or *isn't*.

4 Make sentences a–f negative.
   a It's an interactive whiteboard.
      It isn't an interactive whiteboard.
   b I'm a teacher.
      _____
   c This is a school.
      _____
   d You're from Mexico.
      _____
   e I'm American.
      _____
   f I'm from the UK.
      _____
   g I know your name.
      _____

 Connect

Record yourself saying the phrases on your phone. Send it to a friend or your teacher.

5 ▶1.4 Listen and circle the word you hear.
   a nine   mime
   b Tom   ton
   c note   not
   d number   member
   e an   am
   f car   card
   g pen   ten
   h three   tree
   i card   cat
   j hotel   hospital

a I ____ from Canada.

b I ____ from Chile.

c Tango ____ from Argentina.

d Where ____ you from?

e It ____ a pencil. It ____ a pen.

f It ____ a banana. It ____ an apple.

g It ____ from the U.S. It ____ from Italy.

h It ____ German. It ____ British.

1.4 What's your phone number?

1 ▶1.5 Listen and repeat the picture words and sounds.

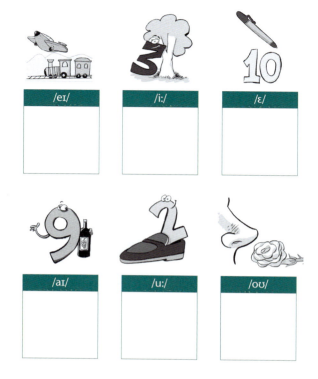

/eɪ/   /iː/   /ɛ/

/aɪ/   /uː/   /oʊ/

2 ▶1.6 Listen and write the letters of the alphabet in the correct boxes in **1**.

📶 Connect
Record yourself saying the words on your phone. Send it to a friend or your teacher.

3 🅐 **Make it personal** Practice saying the letters that are difficult for you.

4 ▶1.7 Listen and write the words you hear.
a _____
b _____
c _____
d _____

5 ▶1.8 Listen and write the phone numbers.
a Jorge _____
b Marina _____
c Mary _____
d Daniel _____
e Amy _____

6 Order the words in a–f to make questions and write them in the table.
a are / Good / you / ? / morning / , / how
b please / What's / ? / name / , / your
c that / , / Spell / please / ?
d you / from / ? / are / Where
e or / single / ? / married / Are / you
f number / telephone / ? / your / What's

a	*Good morning, how are you?*	*Fine, thanks. And you?*
b		
c		
d		
e		
f		

7 ▶1.9 Match the answers to questions a–f and write them in the table in **6**. Listen to check.
☐ It's Rodrigo Sánchez.
a Fine, thanks. And you?
☐ R-O-D-R-I-G-O S-Á-N-C-H-E-Z.
☐ I'm single at the moment.
☐ It's 202-555-0142.
☐ The U.S.

8 🅐 **Make it personal** Read about Veronica and use the model to write your profile.

Hello. My name's Veronica, but my friends call me Nica. I'm from Italy. I'm a student, and I study English in Florence. My address is 22 Via Callata, and my telephone number is 311-0022-5310. I'm not married, I'm single.

_____
_____
_____
_____
_____
_____

1.5 What's your email address?

1 ▶ 1.10 Listen and check the correct email.
   a jenny.nomara@nic.org.iuk
      jeny.namara@mec.org.yuk
      jenny.namara@mec.org.uk
   b claums@pcg.net
      clauns@bct.net
      clauns@pcd.net

2 ▶ 1.11 Listen and complete the information.

```
Name: _____
Nationality: _____
Home address: _____
City: _____
Country: _____
Phone number: _____
Personal email: _____
```

3 🔲 **Make it personal** Read the form and write questions. Then send the questions to a friend and complete the form with his / her answers.
   a What's your name?
   b Where _____
   c _____
   d _____
   e _____
   f _____

```
Name: _____
Home address: _____
_____
Phone number: _____
Personal email: _____
ID number: _____
Vehicle registration number: _____
```

4 Match the columns to make English phrases.
   a Pop   ☐ sorry
   b Good   ☐ me
   c Oh   ☐ day
   d Excuse   ☐ afternoon
   e Have a good ☐ very much
   f Thank you   [a] music

5 Match dialogues a–e to the photos.
   a Night. See you soon!
      Good night, and thanks for a great evening.
   b Bye, everybody! Have a good weekend.
      Bye, Luiza!
   c Hello, Mr. Jackson. How are you today?
      Afternoon, Doctor López. I'm fine, and you?
   d Good morning, Andrew. Nice to meet you.
      Nice to meet you too. Please call me Andy.
   e See you, Erica.
      Bye for now, Antonio!

🔊 **Connect**

Record yourself saying the dialogues on your phone. Send it to a friend or your teacher.

❓ **Can you remember...**
- numbers 1–12?   SB → p. 7
- 6 classroom instructions?   SB → p. 8
- 10 classroom objects?   SB → p. 10
- 10 familiar words in English?   SB → p. 11
- the 26 letters of the alphabet?   SB → p. 12
- 4 Verb *be* – questions?   SB → p. 13
- 10 ways to say hello / goodbye?   SB → p. 15

2 2.1 Are you a student?

1 ▶2.1 Match photos 1–6 to countries a–f. Complete the nationalities and mark the stress. Listen to check.

Sung Lee's Travel Journal

Countries	Nationalities
a Mexico	Mexican
b Chile	
c Canada and the U.S.	
d Argentina	
e Japan	
f Italy	

2 Read and complete the journal with the verb *be*.

My name _____ Sung Lee. I _____ Chinese and I _____ a travel writer. I love to visit new countries. It _____ fantastic. I speak Chinese, Japanese, English, and Spanish. What about you? _____ you a traveler?

3 Order the words to make questions and sentences.
a an / You're / actor .
b a / Are / teacher / you ?
c not / student / a / I'm .
d are / Yes, / you .
e not / I'm / No, .
f from / Are / Brazil / you ?

4 Choose the correct alternatives.
a A: **Are** / **Am** you Spanish?
   B: Yes, I **am** / **are**. **I'm** / **I** from Zaragoza.
b A: **I'm** / **I'm from** Mexican.
   B: No, **you're** / **you** not. You're Venezuelan.
c A: **Am** / **Are** you **a British actor** / **an actor British**?
   B: No, I **not** / **'m not**. I'm from **American** / **the U.S.**

5 ▶2.2 Cross out the word that does *not* have the same sound. Listen to check.

a /w/
   where
   what
   ~~who~~

d /f/
   famous
   Peruvian
   family

b /k/
   actor
   car
   center

e /n/
   American
   politician
   problem

c /m/
   name
   new
   movie

f /t/
   complete
   brother
   eight

6 Write the numbers.
a 13   d 16   g 19
b 14   e 17   h 20
c 15   f 18

2.2 Who's your favorite actor?

1 🅐 **Make it personal** Look at the photos and complete a–c with one of these adjectives.

bad   excellent   fantastic   good   horrible
not very good   OK   incredible   terrible

a This is Bruno Mars.
I think he's _____.

c Ariana Grande!
I think she's _____.

b I think this video game is _____.

2 ▶ 2.3 Order the words to make sentences. Listen to check.

a LeBron James / I / fantastic / a / think / is / basketball player / .
I think LeBron James is a fantastic basketball player.

b horrible / is / movie / *Toy Story 4* / a / .
_____

c actor / think / an / is / excellent / Scarlett Johansson / I / .
_____

d favorite / what's / book / your / ?
_____

e singer / an / Ed Sheeran / is / ok / .
_____

3 Correct one or two mistakes in each of a–e.

a I love the food Mexican.
b It's a movie very good.
c It's a book interesting.
d I think she's a writer excellent.
e I agree. She's a singer terrible.

4 Complete with *he / she / it* and *'s* or *isn't*.

a _____ Marcus Rashford.
_____ a soccer player.
_____ from Britain.
_____ from Germany.

b _____ Taylor Swift.
_____ a politician.
_____ a musician.
_____ from the U.S.

c _____ Hugh Jackman.
_____ an actor and musician.
_____ from Australia.
_____ in New York.
_____ in Sydney, Australia.

d _____ a Mercedes.
_____ a BMW.
_____ a very good car.
_____ from Germany.

e _____ a panda.
_____ a beautiful animal.
_____ from China.

5 🅐 **Make it personal** Write about an actor, movie or sportsperson. Send to your teacher or a classmate.

📶 **Connect**

Find photos of people and items online. Tell your partner what you think of each one.

95

2.3 Is ceviche Mexican?

1 ▶2.4 Listen and check the correct option.

Juan Wow! **Who's / What's** this?
Fran Um, I don't remember her name. Is it Maisie Williams?
Juan Yes, it is. **It's / She's** an incredible actor. I love her movies. *Mary Shelley*, for example, is fantastic! I think **he's / she's** from Australia.
Fran No, she **isn't / not**. **She's / It's** from the UK. **Where's / Who's** the male actor in the movie?
Juan He's Jude Law. **He / He's** a fantastic actor.
Fran Who / How old is he?
Juan I don't know. Around 50?
Fran Hey, Juan, **what's / where's** this?
Juan Oh, it's ceviche. It's fish. It's delicious.
Fran Ceviche? Is **it / he** Mexican?
Juan No, **it / she** isn't. I think **he's / it's** from Peru. It's delicious.
Fran Is it?
Juan Yes, I love **it / he**.

2 ▶2.4 Listen again and answer a–e.
a Who's Maisie Williams?
b Where's she from?
c How old is Jude Law?
d What's ceviche?
e Where's it from?

3 Match questions a–e with responses 1–5.
a How old are you?
b Where is she from?
c Who's Adam Lambert?
d What's feijoada?
e Where's Cali?

1 She's from Mexico.
2 It's in Colombia.
3 It's a delicious Brazilian specialty.
4 I'm 22 today. It's my birthday!
5 He's an American musician.

4 ▶2.5 *Do the quiz!* Listen to check.

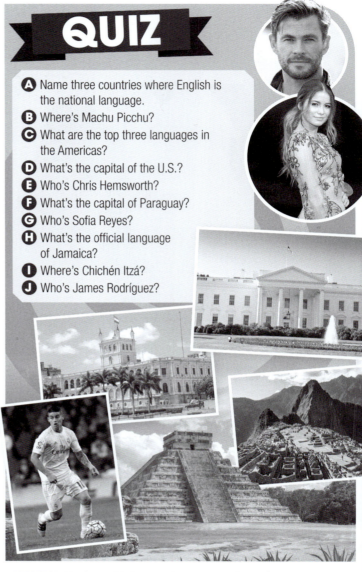

QUIZ

A Name three countries where English is the national language.
B Where's Machu Picchu?
C What are the top three languages in the Americas?
D What's the capital of the U.S.?
E Who's Chris Hemsworth?
F What's the capital of Paraguay?
G Who's Sofia Reyes?
H What's the official language of Jamaica?
I Where's Chichén Itzá?
J Who's James Rodríguez?

Connect

Research online and write four trivia quiz questions. Then test a classmate.

5 Write these lottery numbers. Remember the hyphen!

27 42 68
37 89 51

_____
_____
_____
_____

96

2.4 Where are your two favorite places?

1 Complete a–e with the verb *be* in the correct form.
 a We _____ at home.
 b _____ you happy? Yes, we _____. Very!
 c The people _____ very friendly here.
 d A: _____ they at school?
    B: No, they _____. They _____ at work.
 e We _____ (not) European. _____ Latin American.

2 Rearrange the letters to make adjectives.
 a gib   e tabileufu
 b ewn   f ridneflynu
 c lod   g sipnexven
 d guyl   h hapec

3 Complete a–f with appropriate adjectives from **2**.
 a Ugh, I don't like that sweater. It's _____.
 b It's a horrible place. The people are very _____.
 c Is that a _____ bag? I like it!
 d $150? That's _____ for a dinner!
 e The Temple of Heaven in Beijing is very _____. It's over 600 years old.
 f The view from our window is _____!

4 Rearrange the words to make questions.
 a you / are / home / at ?
 b they / are / friendly ?
 c in / Latin America / we / are / now ?
 d friends / they / good / are / very ?
 e of / from / north / you / are / Spain / the ?
 f expensive / they / an / in / hotel / are ?

5 Complete the answers with the correct form of *be*. Then match them to the questions in **4**.
 1 Yes, they _____. They _____ very nice.
 2 No, we _____. We _____ from Argentina.
 3 Yes, they _____!
 4 No, we _____. We _____ on vacation in Canada at the moment.
 5 Yes, we _____. We _____ Arequipa in the south of Peru.
 6 No, they _____. They _____ in a cheap one. Only $20 a night!

6 🔒 **Make it personal** Answer the questions with your own information.

Are you from Latin America?
Are you a student?
Is your car old?
Are your family in this city?
Are you in a restaurant?
Is the weather good today?

🔊 **Connect**

Record the questions and answers in **6** *and send them to a friend or your teacher.*

2.5 Is English essential for your future?

1. **Reread the text on p. 26 of the Student's Book. True (T) or False (F)?**
   a English is not an important language in the modern world.
   b It's part of the school curriculum in over 1000 countries.
   c One billion people speak or study English globally.
   d It isn't very important in the arts or the media.
   e It's the global language in history.

2. **Complete the questions. Then match them to the answers.**

   a Who _____ Antonio Banderas?
   b How old _____ he?
   c Where _____ he from?
   d _____ he married?
   e And who _____ Venus and Serena Williams?
   f Where _____ they from?

   ☐ I don't know. About 60?
   ☐ No, he's single, I think.
   ☐ They're professional tennis players and sisters.
   ☐ He's a Hollywood actor.
   ☐ They are from the U.S.
   ☐ He's from Spain, but he lives in the U.S.

3. **Circle the different word.**
   a English   Chinese   (Spain)   Portuguese
   b China   Australia Indian   Mexico
   c from   to   in   be
   d web   what   who   where
   e in   the   a   an
   f I   one   you   we
   g are   have   is   am

4. ▶ 2.6 **Listen to two friends playing a guessing game. Who's the person?**

5. ▶ 2.6 **Complete the questions. Listen again to check.**
   Ana Is he American?
   Sam No, he isn't. He's British.
   Ana _____?
   Sam He's around 40.
   Ana _____?
   Sam He's from Bristol in the UK.
   Ana _____?
   Sam Yes, he's very famous. His graffiti is fantastic. I love his art. His initials are RB.
   Ana Oh, I think I know. But I don't remember his name.
   Sam OK, well, his nickname is very famous. The first letter is B. B - A ...
   Ana Ah, OK, it's Ba_____.

6. **Answer true (T) or false (F) about Banksy.**

   a His name's Bill Banks.
   b Sam doesn't know his exact age.
   c He's from Brighton in the UK.
   d He's a famous graffiti artist.

7. 🎧 **Make it personal** Think of another famous person and write six questions and answers about them.

   📶 **Connect**
   Send your questions in 7 to a friend or your teacher. Read their answers. All correct?

   ❓ **Can you remember...**
   - 7 countries and nationalities? SB → p. 18
   - numbers 13–20? SB → p. 19
   - 8 opinion adjectives? SB → p. 21
   - numbers 20–100? SB → p. 23
   - 14 adjectives SB → p. 24

3.1 What do you do?

1 Complete a–h with the jobs, and then match a–h to photos 1–8.

a ☐ o c t d o r
b ☐ v s r r e e
c ☐ a w y r l e
d ☐ g i e n e r e n

e ☐ n e s t t i d
f ☐ d r h r i r s a e s e
g ☐ l e a s c l k s r e
h ☐ c m n i u s a s i

2 ▶3.1 Put the jobs from 1 in the correct stress group. Listen to check.

1 ●●	2 ●●●	3 ●●●	4 ●●●
a teacher	a journalist	a professor	unemployed
	a scientist	a director	

3 ▶3.1 Listen again and repeat the jobs with the suffix -er or -or. Notice the suffix is *not* stressed.

4 ▶3.2 Correct one mistake in each line of the dialogue. Listen to check.
A OK, what's your name and what you do?
B My name's Jane. I'm an unemployed.
A OK. And what do your partner do?
B He's an university professor.
A Right, and what you want to be?
B I want to be bank cashier.

5 **Make it personal** Answer the questions in 4 with your information.

🔊 **Connect**
Record your answers and send them to your teacher or a friend.

99

3.2 Do you have brothers and sisters?

1 Reread the text on p. 34 of the Student's Book and answer a–e. True (T) or false (F)? Correct the false sentences.
   a The name of the family (is) the royal family.
   b The Queen's name's Elizabeth and her husband's name's William.
   c Charles has two children – a boy and a girl.
   d Charlotte is William's only daughter.
   e Charlotte's mother's name's Elizabeth.
   f Her brothers' names are George and Louis.
   g Charles isn't next in line to be king.

2 Circle five more examples of the verb *be* in a–e in **1**.

3 ▶3.3 Which sound is in all words in each line?

mother   brother   son   husband

sister   sibling   children   single

father   family   wife   coffee

Listen and circle the correct picture.

4 Complete Carlos's story with these words.

| children | daughters | husband | mother |
| single | sisters | son | wife |

My father, José, is married to my _____, Marie.
Obviously she's his _____! I'm their only _____.
They have two _____ too, Angela and Sofia. They are my _____. Angela has a _____ and _____.
But I'm _____, and I only have a cat and a dog.

5 Read about Mark's family and answer a–g.

This is my family. I live with my partner and my two children in an apartment in Seattle. My partner, Jessica, is an electrical engineer. She's incredible. My son's name is Gabriel. He's 14 and my daughter's name is Francesca. She's 19. They're both students. They have two pets: Fizz is Gabriel's dog, and Purr is Francesca's cat. I'm Mark. I'm 46 years old, I'm an only child, and I'm a dentist.

   a What's his name? *His name is Mark.*
   b What's his partner's name?
   c What are his children's names?
   d Who or what is Purr?
   e What does Jessica do?
   f What does Mark do?
   g What do their children do?

6 ▶3.4 Write questions for the answers in a–g. Listen, check and repeat.
   a (live / house / apartment)?
       I live in an apartment.
   b (live / alone)?
       No I don't. I live with my partner.
   c (have / children)?
       Yes, I do. I have a son and a daughter.
   d (how old / they)?
       They're 14 and 19.
   e (what / their names)?
       Their names are Francesca and Gabriel.
   f (have / brothers / sisters)?
       No, I'm an only child.
   g (you / married / single)?
       I'm not married, but I live with my partner.

7 ▶3.4 **Make it personal** Listen again and give your own answers.

 Connect

Record your answers and send them to your teacher or a friend.

3.3 Do you have a job?

1 Complete the crossword with the names of workplaces.

Across
1 A teacher works in a …
5 A server works in a …
7 People make things in a …
8 A cashier works in a …
9 A freelancer works at …

Down
2 A doctor works in a …
3 Lawyers and executives work in an …
4 A pharmacist works in a …
6 A travel agent works in a …

2 Match photos a–e to five of the workplaces in **1**.

3 Complete a–f with *in*, *in a*, or *at*.
a My job is fantastic. I'm a singer _____ jazz club.
b I'm a model and I work _____ New York and Milan.
c My sister is a nurse and works _____ private hospital.
d I'm a freelance writer and I work _____ home.
e I'm a secretary and I work _____ modern office downtown.
f He wants to be a chef and work _____ Paris.

4 Order the words in a–g to make questions.
a do / where / study / you / English / ?
_____
b like / you / school / do / your / ?
_____
c work / do / you / where / ?
_____
d you / do / what / do / ?
_____
e want / do / to / you / do / what / ?
_____
f work / do / you / where / want / to / ?
_____
g job / you / do / like / your / ?
_____

5 ▶3.5 Complete the survey with *be* or *do*. Listen to check.

Job Market Survey

❶ What _____ your name? My name _____.
❷ _____ you unemployed?
   a Yes, I am.   b No, I'm not.
❸ _____ you work?
   a Yes, I do.   b No, I don't.
❹ What _____ you do?
   a I'm a student. b I'm a nurse. c I'm a / an _____.
❺ _____ you work freelance?
   a Yes, I do.   b No, I don't.
❻ _____ you work at home?
   a Yes, I do.   b No, I don't.
❼ When _____ you work?
   a In the morning. b In the afternoon. c In the evening.
❽ _____ you like your job?
   a Yes, I do.   b No, I don't.

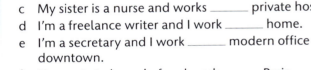

6 🅐 **Make it personal** Reread the survey and write your own answers. Then ask another person the questions.

Connect

Send your answers and your partner's answers to your teacher.

101

3.4 Where does your mother work?

1 Complete the song lines a–f with these verbs.

compares	does	has	loves
makes	wants		

a "She _____ to go home, but nobody's home." (Avril Lavigne)
b "Nothing _____ to you." (Sinéad O'Connor)
c "She _____ diamonds on the inside." (Ben Harper)
d "Every little thing she _____ is magic." (Police)
e "She _____ you yeah yeah yeah!" (The Beatles)
f "You don't know you're beautiful, but that's what _____ you beautiful." (One Direction)

2 🔊 3.6 Read the text about Superman and complete the following table. Listen, reread, and check.

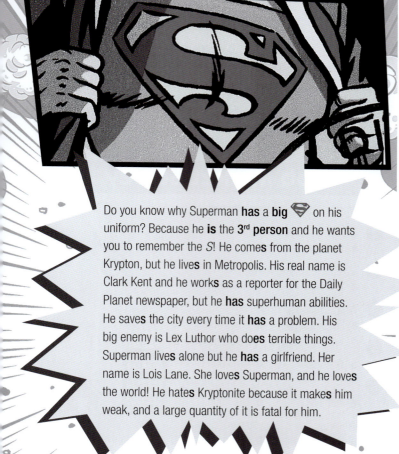

Do you know why Superman **has** a big S on his uniform? Because he **is** the 3rd **person** and he wants you to remember the S! He come**s** from the planet Krypton, but he live**s** in Metropolis. His real name is Clark Kent and he work**s** as a reporter for the Daily Planet newspaper, but he **has** superhuman abilities. He save**s** the city every time it **has** a problem. His big enemy is Lex Luthor who do**es** terrible things. Superman live**s** alone but he **has** a girlfriend. Her name is Lois Lane. She love**s** Superman, and he love**s** the world! He hate**s** Kryptonite because it make**s** him weak, and a large quantity of it is fatal for him.

3rd person	Verb + s	
	comes	from Krypton.
(Superman) He		for a newspaper.
		alone.
		the city.
(Lois) She		Superman.
(Kryptonite) It		him weak.

3 Sentences a–f are false. Make them true.
a Superman lives on Krypton.
  He doesn't live on Krypton, he lives in Metropolis.
b Superman loves Kryptonite.
  _____
c He lives with Lois Lane.
  _____
d He works as a photographer.
  _____
e Lois Lane hates Superman.
  _____
f Superman has a wife.
  _____
g Lex Luthor is his best friend.
  _____

4 Read Gabrielle's email and answer a–c.
a Who is the email to?
b Where is the email from?
c Is the email about a new job or a new home?

Dear Elsa,

Thanks for your message.

I love Mexico, thanks, and I'm very happy in Cancún. It's a beautiful place!

I live in an incredible apartment with my new friends, Hanna and Victor. They're doctors and they work in a local hospital. Victor wants to be a children's doctor, and Hanna wants to work in the emergency room.

I work at the university. I have a small office, and my students are great! I study Spanish before and after work. I don't speak Spanish very well yet, but I love the language!

The people here are friendly, and I love Mexican food too—it's impossible to resist!

I think about you and Italy all the time! Please come and visit, and meet my friends and see this fantastic new city, my new home.

Love,

Gabrielle

5 Reread and answer true (T) or false (F). Correct the false ones.
a Gabrielle doesn't like Cancún.
b Her friends are nurses in the hospital.
c Hanna wants to be a children's doctor.
d Gabrielle works at the university.
e She doesn't study during the week.
f She doesn't like Mexican food.
g She invites Elsa to visit her in Cancún.

📶 **Connect**

Write a similar email about yourself and send it to your teacher or a friend.

3.5 Do you live near here?

1 ▶3.7 Complete the questions. Listen to check.

Matt _____ you live near the office?
Rich Yes, I live with my family in an apartment near the park. Where _____ you live, Matt?
Matt Oh! I live downtown with my cat. Her name is Celia. I adore her!
Rich What? _____ you really like cats? I hate them.
Sarah Really? I love cats. I love all animals.
Matt _____ you have animals, Sarah?
Sarah Yes, I have a dog, and my son has a hamster. What kind of things _____ you like, Rich?
Rich Oh, chocolate, cars, movies, and good wine. I don't like work and I don't like my office!

2 🟢 Make it personal Write five sentences about what you have or don't have in common with them.

Rich lives near his office and I live near my office.
Rich hates cats. I don't hate cats. I love cats.

a _____
b _____
c _____
d _____
e _____

3 ▶3.8 Match a–g to the answers. Listen to check and repeat.

a Do you live alone?
b Do you like animals?
c Do you have brothers and sisters?
d Do you have children?
e Are you married?
f Do you work at the hospital?
g Are you a student?

☐ No, I'm single.
☐ Yes, I am. I study biology.
☐ No, I don't. I work in a school.
☐ No, I live with my family.
☐ Yes, I do. I love them.
☐ Yes, I have a sister.
☐ No, I don't.

4 Order the words in a–d to make dialogues.

a Hi / Clare / , / my / name's / . / meet / you / . / Nice / to
_____

Hello / . / Marge / , / I'm / . / meet / you / Nice / to / too / ,
_____

b or / you / married / Are / single / ?
_____

with / I / my / live / partner / .
_____

see / Oh / , / I / . / coffee / ? / Another
_____

c to / Great / you / . / talking / number / . / Here's / my
_____

Wow / ! / you / Thank / . / Bye / !
_____

d live / here / you / Do / near / ?
_____

I / No / , / don't / . / South Africa / . / live / in / I
_____

you / Cool / ! / Do / city / in / a / live / ?
_____

country / No / . / live / a / in / I / house / don't / , / I / the / in / .
_____

5 ▶3.9 Listen to check. Notice the stressed words.

❓ **Can you remember…**
- 10 jobs? SB → p. 32
- 8 family members? SB → p. 34
- 5 possessive adjectives? SB → p. 34
- 9 places of work? SB → p. 36
- 9 expressions to show interest in conversation? SB → p. 41

4

4.1 Is there an ATM near here?

1 Look at the photos and complete the crossword.

Across

Down

2 Complete a–e with *there*, *is*, or *are*.
a There _____ an umbrella in the office.
b _____ are a lot of doctors in the hospital.
c There _____ five coins in my wallet.
d _____ is a lipstick in my purse.
e There _____ 20 chairs in the classroom.

3 Correct the mistake in each sentence.
a There is two keys on the table.
b Have three notebooks in my bag.
c There are a charger in the office.
d There's four cars on the street.
e Have an umbrella in my car.
f They're three grocery stores near my apartment.

4 Write five sentences with *there is / are* to describe the picture.

___There's a whiteboard on the wall.___
_____
_____
_____
_____

5 ▶4.1 Match pictures 1 and 2 to the underlined sounds below. Listen to check.
☐ Th<u>e</u>se k<u>ey</u>s open th<u>e</u>se doors.
☐ Th<u>i</u>s <u>i</u>s a p<u>i</u>nk l<u>i</u>pst<u>i</u>ck for J<u>i</u>ll.
☐ I like th<u>i</u>s b<u>i</u>g wallet.
☐ Th<u>e</u>se thr<u>ee</u> tr<u>ee</u>s are gr<u>ee</u>n.
☐ G<u>i</u>ve h<u>i</u>m a p<u>i</u>ll s<u>i</u>x times a day.

104

4.2 Are those your books?

1 Complete the comic strips with these lines.

Look, Lurian! What are those?   Oh, no! What's that?   They're cars.
We are here. This is Earth.   No! Jupiter is there!

2 ▶4.2 Match the photos to dialogues a–d. Then circle the correct answer. Listen to check.

a	Ted	Hey, what are **this** / **these**?
	Jessie	**They** / **This** are my Chinese coins.
b	Amanda	Look! **This** / **These** is my new purse.
	Claire	Wow! **They** / **It** is beautiful.
c	Lucy	Monica, what are **this** / **these**? Are **they** / **it** lipsticks?
	Monica	Uh, no! **It** / **They** are my erasers.
d	Chris	Man, is **these** / **this** a tablet?
	Joey	Yeah, **these** / **it** is cool, isn't it?

3 ▶4.3 Correct a mistake in each of a–f. Listen to check.

a W What's ~~these~~? *this*
   M It's a wallet.

b M What's this?
   W It's charger.

c W What's this?
   M They're an umbrella.

d M What are these?
   W It's my keys.

e M What are this?
   W They're cell phones.

f W What's these?
   M They're video games.

4 ▶4.4 Joe and Kim are in a bus station. Read their dialogue and circle the correct option. Listen to check.

Kim Yuk! **This** / **That** is a terrible bus station.
Joe Yeah, I know. **These** / **Those** new terminals are horrible.
Kim Uh-huh! Hey, I think **this** / **that** man over there is your **father** / **mother**.
Joe Yeah, and **these** / **those** boys with him are my **sisters** / **brothers**.
Kim Great. Oh, look! There. **That** / **This** is my bag!
Joe Good. But where **is** / **are** my bags? Uh, excuse me …

5 Complete the colors with the missing vowels.

a gr __ __ n
b gr __ y
c wh __ t __
d bl __ ck
e y __ ll __ w
f bl __ __
g br __ wn
h __ r __ ng __
i p __ nk
j r __ d

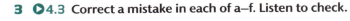

Connect

Find a cool photo online for five of the colors. Send it to a friend or your teacher.

4.3 What things do you lose?

1 ▶ 4.5 Check the two plurals with an extra syllable, /ɪz/. Listen to check.
   a backpack _____
   b ball _____
   c candy _____
   d car _____
   e cell phone _____
   f computer _____
   g dictionary _____
   h ring _____
   i sunglass _____
   j umbrella _____
   k video game _____
   l watch _____

2 ▶ 4.6 Complete a–f with six words from 1, singular or plural, depending on the context. Listen to check.
   a Wow! I love your _____. Does it take good photos?
   b Look at those diamond _____. They're beautiful.
   c I don't like chocolate _____.
   d These _____ are cool. They're my new Ray Bans!
   e My _____ is very heavy. It's full of books.
   f I have three _____, but all show different times.

3 **Make it personal** Read the example. Which of the items in 1 do you have at home?
   I have an umbrella at home, but there are no dictionaries. I only have one backpack.

   Connect
   Record your answer and send it to a friend.

4 Correct the mistakes in a–i. Be careful! Two sentences are correct.
   a There is two bananas on the table.
   b My notebooks is on my backpack.
   c There are tablets on the school?
   d There is a cat in the box.
   e There are dictionaries in your classroom?
   f There is a flash drive on your office?
   g There are two taxis in front of my house.
   h Have an umbrella in my car.
   i There are good soccer players in your school?

5 Write the time under each clock.

4.4 What time do you get up?

1 Match verbs 1–5 to words a–e.

1 have
2 get
3 go to
4 check
5 leave

a bed / the gym
b my phone
c breakfast / lunch / dinner
d home
e up

2 Write the names of the activities in **1** under pictures 1–8.

1 _____

2 _____

3 _____

4 _____

5 _____

6 _____
7 _____

3 The pictures in **2** show Carla's typical day. Write a sentence for each picture.

1 *Carla gets up at six a.m.*
2 _____
3 _____
4 _____
5 _____
6 _____
7 _____
8 _____

4 🎤 **Make it personal** What time do you do each of the things in Exercise 3?

📶 **Connect**

*Send your answers in **4** to your teacher or a friend.*

8 _____

107

4.5 How do you pronounce *meme* in English?

1 ○ 4.7 Read the information and order the events, 1–5. Listen to check.

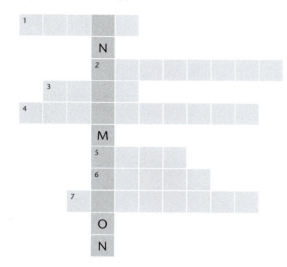

Snapchat is a photo- and video-sharing app people use to communicate with friends and family. People can share photos, videos, and "stories" but only for a short time. Then they disappear.

In November 2012, people share twenty million photos a day. ☐

Three students at Stanford University have an idea for an app which shares photos for a short time before they disappear. ☐

There are now nearly 20 million users of Snapchat around the world. ☐

They create the app, first called Picaboo for iOS in July 2011. They start it again in September 2011 and call it Snapchat. ☐

They create "Lenses," or video filters, which people can use to change how they look, in January 2015. ☐

2 Answer a–d. Reread to check.
 a How old is Snapchat?
 b How many students created it?
 c How many people use it?
 d Is Snapchat the original name of the app?

Connect

Send your answers to questions 1–3 to your teacher or a friend.
1 Do you use Snapchat?
2 How many friends do you have on Snapchat / other social networks?
3 Do you use any other social networks?

3 Complete the crossword with the missing technology words. What's the secret word in gray? (Clue: it's a type of technology)

```
         N
         2
      3
   4
         M
         5
         6
      7
         O
         N
```

1 a way of sending messages electronically
2 one of the first social networks
3 an online diary
4 technology that you have in your bag or purse
5 software programs for mobile devices
6 a message you post on *Twitter*
7 a thousand megabytes

Can you remember...
- 10 personal objects?   SB → p. 44
- 4 demonstrative pronouns?   SB → p. 46
- 10 colors?   SB → p. 47
- 6 more objects?   SB → p. 48
- 10 daily activities?   SB → p. 50
- pronunciation of the pink-stressed technology words?   SB → p. 52

108

5.1 Do you drink a lot of coffee?

1 Find these ten food items in the wordsearch.

M	H	N	R	Z	Q	W	U	S	O	Z	Y
E	U	U	Z	B	E	A	N	S	R	P	O
A	V	Q	I	V	H	R	G	S	M	X	R
T	L	A	T	A	B	V	I	C	I	Q	A
C	V	F	E	U	R	A	X	M	L	S	N
S	H	T	A	O	O	N	S	I	K	T	G
C	H	E	E	S	E	U	O	O	T	L	E
H	W	N	K	R	U	E	F	G	A	F	J
O	V	S	N	M	N	K	T	M	G	L	U
E	G	G	S	F	F	P	D	A	W	S	I
Q	D	R	T	Y	C	T	R	M	E	K	C
T	C	O	A	V	J	Y	I	M	E	G	E
S	C	O	F	F	E	E	N	R	E	X	B
X	D	W	Y	O	G	G	K	O	Y	R	Q
Q	B	R	E	A	D	E	S	M	S	J	S

2 Read the puzzle and guess the six food items.

a It's a liquid. It's white. It's good with cereal and coffee.
☐☐☐☐

b It comes from an animal. We cook it before we eat it.
☐☐☐☐

c It's a liquid. It's black. We usually drink it hot.
☐☐☐☐☐☐

d They are natural and usually sweet. We make juice with them.
☐☐☐☐☐☐

e There are many colors and types of these. We eat them hot or cold in a salad.
☐☐☐☐☐☐☐☐

f They are liquid, have many colors, and contain no alcohol. People usually drink them with snacks or meals.
☐☐☐☐ ☐☐☐☐☐

3 ▶5.1 Circle the words with a different vowel sound. Listen to check.

a fruit
   lunch
   juice   /uː/

c bread
   egg
   eat    /ɛ/

b bread
   meat
   beans   /iː/

d wine
   milk
   drink   /ɪ/

4 ▶5.2 Listen to a journalist. Circle the 10 words you hear. Then match photos a–d to four of the food items and mark the stress.

bread	butter	chocolate	coffee
croissants	eggs	fish	fruit
meat	orange juice	pancakes	potatoes
rice	soup	tea	vegetables

5 ▶5.2 Listen again. True (T) or false (F)?
a Americans eat pancakes for breakfast.
b Japanese and Korean people usually eat eggs.
c In France, people eat croissants with milk.
d Brazilians usually drink coffee for breakfast.
e Rice isn't a breakfast item globally.

6 🎤 **Make it personal** Order the words in a–e to make questions and answer them.
a the / is / favorite / of / what / meal / your / day / ?
b of / eat / lot / meat / you / do / ?
c do / what / for / lunch / you / have / ?
d there / lot / a / vegetables / your / are / house / in / of / ?
e have / coffee / do / in / you / sugar / your / ?
f eat / lot / do / snacks / you / a / of / ?

📶 **Connect**

Record your answers and send them to a friend.

109

5.2 What's your favorite food?

1 Reread the food words on p. 60 in the Student's Book. Then do the food quiz in two minutes.
   a What fruit starts with the letter G?
   b What meat starts with B?
   c Name a fruit that starts with O and is a color too.
   d What fast food starts with P?
   e What vegetable starts with C?
   f We use potatoes to make them. They start with F.
   g It starts with L and it's green.

2 ▶5.3 Match photos a–h to the food items. Then listen and put the words in the correct column. Which word doesn't go in any of the columns?

☐ bananas   ☐ kiwi
☐ chicken   ☐ potatoes
☐ fish   ☐ tomatoes
☐ hamburger   ☐ vegetables

3 Use the prompts to write sentences / questions.
   a my sister / love / chicken.
      My sister loves chicken.
   b you / like / grapes?
      _____
   c My children / (not) like / carrots.
      _____
   d Graeme / hate / fish.
      _____
   e my dad / love / bananas.
      _____
   f Phil / like / pasta?
      _____
   g Andrea / (not) like / beef.
      _____

4 Correct the mistakes in a–f.
   a My father like chicken a lot.
   b His brother and sister not like fish.
   c My mother really don't like hamburgers.
   d My sister doesn't likes tomatoes?
   e I not eat meat, I'm a vegetarian.
   f What food items you like?

5 **Make it personal** *My food!* Complete the text about your eating habits.

I usually eat _____ meals a day. My favorite meal is _____ and I like to eat _____. I don't like _____. For breakfast I have _____ and I usually drink _____. My favorite snacks are _____ and I love _____ very much.

Connect

Record the completed text and send it to your teacher or a friend. Illustrate your favorite foods too!

●●●	●●	●●●
professor	*breakfast*	

5.3 What do you usually do on Friday evenings?

1 ▶5.4 Order the letters to make the days of the week a–g, and put them in the correct order. Listen to check.

a urdhaTsy
b odyMna
c arSytuad
d dySuan
e ndesayWde
f uedyaTs
g riFyad

1	Sunday
2	
3	
4	
5	
6	
7	

2 ▶5.5 Read the article. True (T) or false (F)? Listen to check.

WEEKENDS AROUND THE WORLD

Different countries have different weekends. In Europe and the Americas, the weekend consists of Saturday and Sunday. Monday to Friday is called the workweek.
In other countries, especially in the Middle East (countries like Israel, Egypt, Jordan, and Iraq), the weekend starts on Thursday or Friday, and ends on Saturday. People work from Sunday to Thursday.
In certain countries, Saudi Arabia, Afghanistan, and Oman, for example, the weekend is Thursday and Friday and the workweek is Saturday to Wednesday.
But Monday is always a workday. Maybe that's why there are a lot of negative songs about it: "Monday Monday," "I Don't Like Mondays," "Just Another Manic Monday," and the best one we know, "Blue Monday" by New Order!

Oh, no! Monday again!

a People don't usually work on Saturday or Sunday in Europe.
b Tuesday and Wednesday are part of the workweek in Central America and Eastern Europe.
c People always work on Friday in Israel.
d Sunday is never a workday in Saudi Arabia.
e Monday is a workday all over the world.

3 Order the words in posts a–f to make sentences.

Talk About Your Week!

A Lisa
Friday's / favorite / my / of / the / day / week

B Derek
to / on Sunday / usually / go / I / don't / church

C Susan
Monday / partner / hates / my / mornings

D Ramon
to / sometimes / gym / on weekends / I / go / the

E Marshal
shopping / always / my / on Saturday / I / wife / together / and / go

F Isabelle
the / watch / never / evening / in / we / TV

4 🔵 Make it personal Check the sentences in **3** that are true for you. Rewrite the others to make them true for you.

5 Complete the table with *never, sometimes, usually,* and *always*.

Adverbs

0%   50%   80%   100%

6 🔵 Make it personal Insert adverbs from **5** into a–e to make true sentences.

a I read books in my language.
b I read online in English.
c I buy food at the same grocery store.
d I go to restaurants with my family on weekends.
e In the evenings I listen to music and watch TV.

7 Complete a–e with *in* or *on*.

a I have French classes ____ Monday and Wednesday mornings.
b My best friend and I go to ballet class ____ the evenings.
c I take my daughter to soccer practice ____ Fridays.
d My brother and I usually play video games ____ the morning before school.
e I always study online ____ Thursday afternoons.

111

5.4 Do you like Rihanna's music?

1 🎤 **Make it personal** Match the names and possessions and give your opinion.

Iron man	food		fantastic
Gabriel García Márquez	inventions	is	terrible
Leonardo da Vinci	suit		excellent
Banksy	movies	are	good
Jamie Oliver	art		boring
Martin Scorsese	books		interesting

a *Iron man's suit is fantastic.*
b _____
c _____
d _____
e _____
f _____

2 ▶ 5.6 Listen and match extracts a–d to the photos.

flowery shirt

Van Gogh exhibition

the Golden Boot

Shakira

3 ▶ 5.6 Listen again and complete the stories with these names + 's.

Lewis Hamilton   Harry Kane
Shakira   Van Gogh

_____ best work—but only for 28 days!
← reply   🔁 retweet   ★ favourite

_____ baby boy.
Congratulations to Mom and Dad.

_____ Golden Boot—fantastic!
← reply   🔁 retweet   ★ favourite

_____ flowery shirt divides opinion!

4 Which sentence is correct? Circle the correct option.
a The White House is **the U.S. President official's residence** / **the U.S. President's official residence**.
b **Adele's songs** / **The songs of Adele's** are beautiful.
c **Shakira's son's name's** / **Shakira son's name** Milan.
d *Sunflowers* is one of **Van Gogh famous' paintings** / **Van Gogh's famous paintings**.

5 Circle the correct pronoun.
a What do you think of Leonardo DiCaprio?
    I don't like **him** / **it** / **her**.
b Do you like Billie Eilish?
    Yes, I do. I like **him** / **it** / **her** a lot.
c Do you like Maroon 5?
    No, I don't like **him** / **them** / **they**. I prefer rock music!
d What do you think of basketball?
    I love **them** / **him** / **her** / **it**. To watch and to play!

6 🎤 **Make it personal** Rewrite questions a–f and answer them.
a your / name / mother's / what / 's / ?
   _____
b what / best friend's / your / job / 's / ?
   _____
c favorite / singer / your / who / 's / ?
   _____
d what / 's / movie / your / favorite / ?
   _____
e Jessica Alba / what / you / do / think / of / ?
   _____

📶 **Connect**

Record your answers and send them to a friend.

5.5 Do you eat a lot of fast food?

1 Find eight food and drink items in the puzzle. Circle the words with the same spelling in your language.

frenchfriescheeseburgerpizzavanillamilkshakehotdogsaladchocolateicecreamyogurt

2 Use the items in **1** to complete Sara's email.

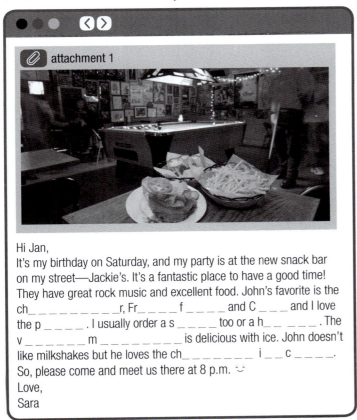

attachment 1

Hi Jan,
It's my birthday on Saturday, and my party is at the new snack bar on my street—Jackie's. It's a fantastic place to have a good time! They have great rock music and excellent food. John's favorite is the ch _ _ _ _ _ _ _ _ r, Fr _ _ _ _ f _ _ _ _ and C _ _ _ and I love the p _ _ _ _. I usually order a s _ _ _ _ too or a h _ _ _ _ _. The v _ _ _ _ _ _ _ m _ _ _ _ _ _ _ _ _ is delicious with ice. John doesn't like milkshakes but he loves the ch _ _ _ _ _ _ _ _ i _ _ c _ _ _ _.
So, please come and meet us there at 8 p.m. ☺
Love,
Sara

3 ▶5.7 Listen and circle the word that *doesn't* have the sound from the pictures.

a	🪑	**chocolate**	school	**cheese**	French
b	🏺	milk	vanilla	ice	music
c	👨‍💼	ham	small	snack	salad
d	📱	pizza	fries	ice	my
e	🌳	cream	cheese	pizza	like

4 🗣 **Make it personal** Answer a–d.
a Do you usually eat special food or go to a special place to eat on your birthday?
b Name three snack bar items you love.
c What are your favorite three drinks?
d Name three food items you don't like.

5 ▶5.8 Order the dialogue, a–h. Listen to check.
☐ A large cola with ice, please.
☐ Anything else?
☐ Yes. A cheeseburger and some French fries, please.
☐ Can I help you?
☐ Right. For here or to go?
☐ Here you are. A cheeseburger, French fries, and a cola.
☐ Thanks.
☐ For here.

6 ▶5.9 Check the best answer. Listen to check.
1 Hi. Are you ready to order?
  a Yes, please. A tomato pasta.
  b No. That's all, thank you.
2 Anything to drink?
  a Yes, a small one.
  b Yes, a medium cola, please.
3 Hello, can I help you?
  a A chocolate ice cream, please.
  b Chocolate ice cream.
4 For here or to go?
  a Yes, please.
  b To go, please.
5 With ice?
  a No French fries, thanks.
  b No, thank you.
6 Large, medium, or small?
  a Small, please.
  b Yes, please.

❓ **Can you remember…**
- 4 meals? SB ➔ p. 58
- 12 food and drink words? SB ➔ p. 58
- 16 food words? SB ➔ p. 60
- the 7 days of the week? SB ➔ p. 62
- 7 weekend activities? SB ➔ p. 62
- 4 object pronouns? SB ➔ p. 65
- 5 fast food words? SB ➔ p. 67

Audioscript

Unit 1

◉ 1.4
a Let's play a **mime** game. Oh yeah!
b This is my friend **Tom**.
c Read this **note** for me.
d What's your phone **number**?
e I **am** Carlos. Nice to meet you.
f My **car** is from China.
g What's this in English? It's a **pen**.
h This is a beautiful **tree**.
i This is Molly, my **cat**.
j Wow! This is our **hotel**!

◉ 1.5
plane, train, /eɪ/
three, tree, /iː/
pen, ten, /ɛ/
nine, wine /aɪ/
shoe, two /uː/
nose, rose /oʊ/

◉ 1.8
J = Jorge   M1 = Marina   M2 = Mary   D = Daniel
A = Amy
J   Hi! This is Jorge. You can call me at four, six, two, eight, three, one, double seven, three. OK? That's four, six, two, eight, three, one, double seven, three. Thanks.
M1 Oh, hello! You can phone me at nine, one, eight, four, double three. That's nine, one, eight, four, double three. Bye.
M2 Hi. It's Mary! Seven, double oh, one, double five, one, two. That's seven, double oh, one, double five, one, two.
D   Call Daniel at this number: double oh, double four, six, one, seven, eight, two. See you later. Don't forget the number. Double oh, double four, six, one, seven, eight, two.
A   Four, one, double six, nine, eight, three. It's Amy. Four, one, double six, nine, eight, three. Call me!

◉ 1.9
I = interviewer   R = Rodrigo
I   Good morning. How are you?
R   Fine, thanks. And you?
I   Very well, thank you. What's your name, please?
R   It's Rodrigo Sánchez.
I   Spell that, please.
R   R-O-D-R-I-G-O S-A-N-C-H-E-Z
I   Where are you from?
R   The United States.
I   Are you married or single?
R   I'm single at the moment.
I   What's your telephone number?
R   It's 202 – 555 – 0142
I   Thank you very much for your time, Mr. Sánchez. My company appreciates your …

◉ 1.10
S = secretary   J = Jenny   C = Claudio
a   S   Jenny, what's your email address?
    J   It's jenny.namara@mec.org.uk.
    S   Spell that, please.
    J   It's J-E-N-N-Y dot N-A-M-A-R-A at M-E-C dot org dot U-K.
b   S   So, Claudio, what's your email address?
    C   Right. It's clauns@bct.net.
    S   Spell that, please.
    C   C-L-A-U-N-S at B-C-T dot net. OK?

◉ 1.11
I = interviewer   A = Alfredo
I   Can you tell me your name, please?
A   Certainly. It's Alfredo Giardelli.
I   Thank you. Can you spell that for me, please?
A   Certainly. It's A-L-F-R-E-D-O G-I-A-R-D-E double L-I.
I   And where are you from, Alfredo?
A   I'm Argentinian.
I   And what's your address?
A   3055 West 78th Street, Boston. In the U.S.
I   Thank you very much. And can you tell me your telephone number?
A   00 1901 555 7422.
I   And finally, Alfredo, your email address?
A   Uh-huh. My personal email is alfredogi@id2.com, that's A-L-F-R-E-D-O-G-I at I-D-2 dot com.
I   Thank you. Now, what we want Alfredo is…

Unit 2

◉ 2.4
J = Juan   F = Fran
J   Wow! Who's this?
F   Um, I don't remember her name. Is it Maisie Williams?
J   Yes, it is. She's an incredible actor. I love her movies. *Mary Shelley*, for example, is fantastic! I think she's from Australia.
F   No, she isn't. She's from the UK. Who's the male actor in the movie?
J   He's Jude Law. He's a fantastic actor.
F   How old is he?
J   I don't know. Around 50?
F   Hey Juan, what's this?
J   Oh, it's ceviche. It's fish. It's delicious.
F   Ceviche? Is it Mexican?
J   No, it isn't. I think it's from Peru. It's delicious.
F   Is it?
J   Yes, I love it.

◉ 2.5
H = TV host   M = Melissa   J = Jacob
H   So, letter a. Three countries where English is the national language.
M   The USA, the UK and… uh… Canada.
H   Very good, Melissa. Question b. Where's Machu Picchu?
M   It's in Peru.
H   Correct! Melissa again! Question c: What are the top three languages in the Americas?
J   Uh, English, Spanish, and… uh, Portuguese.
H   Excellent, Jacob. Next question. What's the capital of the U.S.?
M   It's Washington, D.C.
H   Great! Question e. Who's Chris Hemsworth?
J   He's an actor, yeah, an Australian actor.
H   Yes! F. What's the capital of Paraguay?
J   It's Asunción.
H   Very good! Question g. Who's Sofia Reyes?
M   She's a Mexican singer and actor.
H   Correct! Now, question h. What's the official language of Jamaica?
J   It's English!
H   Yes! Question i. Where's Chichén Itzá?
M   It's in Yucatan, uh, in Mexico.
H   Excellent, Melissa. Last question. Who's James Rodríguez?
M   He's, uh, a Colombian soccer player.
H   Melissa again! Very good! And the winner is…

◉ 2.6
A = Ana   S = Sam
A   Is he American?
S   No, he isn't. He's British.
A   How old is he?
S   He's around 40.
A   Where's he from?
S   He's from Bristol in the UK.
A   Is he famous?
S   Yes, he's very famous. His graffiti is fantastic. I love his art. His initials are RB.
A   Oh, I think I know. But I don't remember his name.
S   OK, well, his nickname is very famous. The first letter is B. B - A…
A   Ah, OK, it's Ba.....

Audioscript

Unit 3

3.5
MR = market researcher J = Joshua
MR Excuse me, hello! Can I ask you some questions about your job?
J Oh, hi. Uh, sure.
MR Uh, what's your name?
J My name's Joshua.
MR Uh, Joshua, are you unemployed?
J No, I'm not.
MR Uhm, uh, so, do you work?
J Yes, I do.
MR And, uh, what do you do?
J I'm an engineer.
MR Um, OK. Do you work freelance?
J No, I don't.
MR Do you work at home?
J No, I don't...
MR Uhm, when do you work?
J Ha! In the morning, in the afternoon and the evening!
MR Oh, uh, OK. And... do you like your job?
J Yes, I do.
MR Uh, great. Thanks.
J No problem.

3.7
M=Matt R=Rich S=Sarah
M Do you live near the office?
R Yes, I live with my family in an apartment near the park. Where do you live, Matt?
M Oh! I live downtown with my cat. Her name is Celia. I adore her!
R What? Do you really like cats? I hate them.
S Really? I love cats. I love all animals.
M Do you have animals, Sarah?
S Yes, I have a dog, and my son has a hamster. What kind of things do you like, Rich?
R Oh, chocolate, cars, movies, and good wine. I don't like work and I don't like my office!

3.8
A Do you live alone?
B No, I live with my family.
A Do you like animals?
B Yes, I do. I love them.
A Do you have brothers and sisters?
B Yes, I have a sister.
A Do you have children?
B No, I don't.
A Are you married?
B No, I'm single.
A Do you work at the hospital?
B No, I don't, I work in a school.
A Are you a student?
B Yes, I am. I study biology.

Unit 4

4.2
T=Ted J=Jessie A=Amanda C=Claire L=Lucy
M=Monica Ch = Chris Jo = Joey
a T Hey, what are these?
  J They are my Chinese coins.
b A Look! This is my new purse.
  C Wow! It is beautiful.
c L Monica, what are these? Are they lipsticks?
  M Uh, no! They are my erasers.
d Ch Man, is this a tablet?
  Jo Yeah, it is cool, isn't it?

4.4
J=Joe K=Kim
K Yuk! This is a terrible bus station.
J Yeah, I know. These new terminals are horrible.
K Uh-huh! Hey, I think that man over there is your father.
J Yeah, and those boys with him are my brothers.
K Great. Oh, look! There. That is my bag!
J Good. But where are my bags? Uh, excuse me ...

4.7
Snapchat is a photo- and video-sharing app people use to communicate with friends and family. People can share photos, videos, and "stories" for a short time. Then they disappear.
Three students at Stanford University have an idea for an app which shares photos for a short time before they disappear.
They create the app, first called Picaboo for iOS in July 2011. They start it again in September 2011 and call it Snapchat.
In November 2012, people share twenty million photos a day.
They create "Lenses," or video filters, which people can use to change how they look, in January 2015. There are now nearly twenty million users of Snapchat around the world.

Unit 5

5.2
As we all know, it's important to be healthy and breakfast is a very important meal. What do people eat for breakfast around the world? In the U.S., people often drink orange juice and usually eat pancakes with fruit. In some countries – Japan and South Korea, for example – soup and rice are very common for breakfast. The French usually eat croissants, sometimes with chocolate in it! In Brazil, bread with butter and coffee are considered the ideal breakfast. Well, all this talk of food has made me hungry, so I'll hand you back to the studio and on the show next week ...

5.6
A ... here for four weeks only. A fantastic opportunity to see Vincent Van Gogh's fabulous paintings.
B ... hahaha. And, congratulations, Shakira, too—a new baby boy. Milan! What an, uh, interesting name!
C And congratulations Harry Kane! The FIFA Golden Boot. What a fantastic soccer player!
D And here's an interesting story about Lewis Hamilton and his flowery shirt. Yes, really, a flowery shirt! My daughter loves it—but, uh, I'm not sure.

5.8
S=server C=customer
S Can I help you?
C Yes. A cheeseburger and some French fries, please.
S Anything else?
C A large cola with ice, please.
S Right. For here or to go?
C For here.
S Here you are. A cheeseburger, French fries, and a cola.
C Thanks.

115

Answer Key

Unit 1

1.1
1 **Receptionist** I'm / My name is
  Student I'm / My name is, Nice to meet you, call me
2 Name: Francesca Lima
3 Personal answers.
4 d, a, b, c
5 c, d, a, b
6 a one   b ten   c seven   d nine   e four
  f six   g twelve   h two   i eleven   j five
7 a seven, nine   b twelve   c eight, ten
  d five, three   e seven, six

1.2
1 a **Listen to** the dialogue.   b **Look at** the photo.
  c **Read** the text.   d **Repeat** the sentence.
  e **Complete** the exercise.
2 a Please read the text and listen **to** the CD.
  b Now look **at** the picture and match the columns.
  c Look **at** the picture and complete the dialogue.
3 e, c, b, f, d, g
4 a What's / What is your name?   b Where are you from?   c What's / What is your address?
  d What's / What is your telephone number?

1.3
1 a a   b an   c a   d a   e an   f a   g a
  h a   i a   j an
2 1 c   2 f   3 d   4 a   5 g   6 h
3 a 'm   b 'm   c 's   d are   e isn't / 's
  f isn't / 's   g isn't / 's   h isn't / 's
4 b I'm not a teacher.   c This isn't a school.
  d You aren't from Japan.
  e I'm not American.   f I'm not from the UK.
5 a mime   b Tom   c note   d number   e am
  f car   g pen   h tree   i cat   j here

1.4
2 /eɪ/ A, H, J, K   /uː/ Q, U, W
  /iː/ B, C, D, E, G, P, T,   /oʊ/ O
       V, Z   /ɑ/ R (box not
  /ɛ/ F, L, M, N, S, X   included)
  /aɪ/ I, Y
3 Personal answers.
4 a Eraser   b Notebook   c Chair   d Restaurant
5 a 462831773   d 004461782
  b 918433   e 4166983
  c 70015512
6 a Good morning. How are you?
  b What's your name, please?
  c Spell that, please.
  d Where are you from?
  e Are you married or single?
  f What's your telephone number?
7 b, a, c, e, f, d
8 Personal answers.

1.5
1 a jenny.namara@mec.org.uk
  b clauns@bct.net
2 Name: Alfredo Giardelli
  Nationality: Argentinian
  Home address: 3055 West 78th Street
  City: Boston
  Country: the USA
  Phone number: 00 1901 555 7422
  Personal email: alfredogi@id2.com
3 b do you live?   c What's your phone number?
  d What's your personal email?
  e What's your ID number?
  f What's your vehicle registration number? Personal answers.

4 c, d, e, b, f
5 c, d, b, a, e

Unit 2

2.1
1 1 f / Italy / Italian
  2 d / Argentina / Argentinian
  3 e / Japan / Japanese
  4 a / Mexico / Mexican
  5 c / Canada and the U.S. / Canadian and American
  6 b / Chile / Chilean
2 's/is, 'm/am, 'm/am, 's/is, Are
3 a You're an actor.   d Yes, you are.
  b Are you a teacher?   e No, I'm not.
  c I'm not a student.   f Are you from Brazil?
4 a Are, am   b you're   c Are, 'm
5 a who   b center   c new
  d Peruvian   e from
6 a thirteen   b fourteen   c fifteen
  d sixteen   e seventeen   f eighteen
  g nineteen   h twenty

2.2
1 Personal answers.
2 b *Toy Story 4* is a horrible movie.
  c I think Scarlett Johansson is an excellent actor.
  d What's your favorite book?
  e Ed Sheeran is an OK singer.
3 a I love **Mexican** food.
  b It's **very good movie**.
  c It's **an interesting book**.
  d I think she's **an excellent writer**.
  e I agree. She's a **terrible singer**.
4 a He's, he's, he's   b She's, she's, she's
  c He's, he's, he's   d It's, it's, it's
  e It's, it's, it's
5 Personal answers

2.3
1 Who's, She's, she's, isn't, She's, Who's, He's, what's, it, it, it's, it.
2 a She's an actor.   b She's from the UK.
  c He's an actor.   d It's a dish.   e It's from Peru.
3 a 4   b 1   c 5   d 3   e 2
4 a Possible answers: The U.S., the UK, and Canada.
  b It's in Peru.
  c They are English, Spanish, and Portuguese.
  d It's Washington, D.C.   e He's an actor.
  f It's Asunción.
  g She's a Mexican singer and actor.
  h It's English.   i It's in Mexico.
  j He's a Colombian soccer player.
5 twenty-seven, thirty-seven, forty-two, eighty-nine, sixty-eight, fifty-one.

2.4
1 a 're/are   b Are   c are
  d Are, aren't, 're/are.   e aren't/'re not
2 a big   b new   c old
  d ugly   e beautiful   f unfriendly
  g expensive   h cheap
3 a ugly   b unfriendly   c new
  d expensive   e old   f beautiful
4 a Are you at home?   d Are they good
  b Are they friendly?   friends?
  c Are we nearly there?   e Are you from Spain?
  f Are they in an expensive hotel?
5 1 are, 're/are (b)   2 aren't, 're/are (e)
  3 are (d)   4 aren't, 're/are (a)
  5 are (c)   6 aren't, 're/are (f)
6 Personal answers.

2.5
1 a F   b T   c F   d F   e T
2 a 's/is   b is   c 's/is   d Is   e are   f are
  b, d, e, a, f, c
3 b Indian   c be   d web   e in   f one   g have
4 Banksy
5 **Ana** How old is he?
  Ana Where's he from?
  Ana Is he famous?
  Ana Banksy
6 a F   b T   c F   d T
7 Personal questions and answers.

Unit 3

3.1
1 a 8 / She's a doctor   e 2 / She's a dentist.
  b 6 / He's a server.   f 4 / She's a hairdresser.
  c 1 / He's a lawyer.   g 3 / She's a sales clerk.
  d 5 / She's an engineer.   h 7 / He's a musician.
2 1 a dentist / a doctor / a lawyer / a sales clerk / a server
  2 a hairdresser   3 a musician   4 an engineer
4 A OK, what's your name and what **do** you do?
  B My name's Jane. I'm unemployed.
  A OK. And what **does** your partner do?
  B He's **a** university professor.
  A Right, and what **do** you want to be?
  B I want to be **a** bank cashier.
5 Personal answers.

3.2
1 a T   b F. Her husband's name's Philip.
  c T   d F. Her mother's name's Kate.   e T
2 name's, name's, **is**, name's, **are**
3 a /ʌ/ sun, run, mother, brother, son, husband
  b /ɪ/ six, mix, sister, sibling, children, single
  c /f/ fish, feet, father, family, wife, coffee
4 mother, wife, son, daughters, sisters, husband, children, single
5 b His partner's name's Jessica.
  c His daughter's name's Francesca.
  d Mark's son's name's Gabriel.
  e She's an engineer.
  f Mark is a dentist.
  g They're both students.
6 a Do you live in a house or an apartment?
  b Do you live alone?   c Do you have children?
  d How old are they?   e What are their names?
  f Do you have brothers and sisters?
  g Are you married or single?
7 Personal answers.

3.3
1 **Across**   **Down**
  1 school   9 home   2 hospital
  5 restaurant   3 office
  7 factory   4 drugstore
  8 bank   6 travel agency
2 a a factory   b an office   c a bank
  d a drugstore   e a restaurant
3 a in a   b in c   in a   d at   e in a   f in
4 a Where do you study English?
  b Do you like your school?
  c Where do you work?
  d What do you do?
  e What do you want to do?
  f Where do you want to work?
  g Do you like your job?
5 1 's, 's (is)   2 Are (b No, I'm not.)
  3 Do (a Yes, I do.)   4 do (c I'm an **engineer**.)
  5 Do (b No, I don't.) 6 Do (b No, I don't.)
  7 do (a In an office.) 8 Do (a Yes, I do.)
6 Personal answers.

116

Answer Key

3.4
1 a wants   b compares   c has   d does
  e loves   f makes

2
3rd person	Verb + s	
(Superman) He	comes	from Krypton.
(Superman) He	works	for a newspaper.
He	lives	alone.
He	saves	the city.
(Lois) She	loves	Superman.
(Kryptonite) It	makes	him weak.

3 b Superman doesn't love Kryptonite.
  c He doesn't live with Lois Lane.
  d He doesn't work as a photographer.
  e Lois Lane doesn't hate Superman.
  f Superman doesn't have a wife.
4 a The email is to Elsa.
  b The email is from Mexico.
  c The email is about a new home.
5 a F   b T   c F   d T   e T   f F

3.5
1 Do, do, Do, Do, do
2 Personal answers.
3 e, g, f, a, b, c, d
4 a Hi, my name's Clare. Nice to meet you.
    Hello, I'm Marge. Nice to meet you too.
  b Are you married or single?
    I live with my partner.
    Oh, I see. Another coffee?
  c Here's my number. Great talking to you. or Great
    talking to you. Here's my number.
    Wow! Thank you. Bye!
  d Do you live near here?
    No, I don't. I live in South Africa.
    Cool! Do you live in a city?
    No, I don't. I live in a house in the country.

Unit 4

4.1
1 Across   Down
  1 umbrella   8 comb   2 lipstick
  4 keys   10 charger   3 pills
  5 wallet   7 ID Card
  6 coins   b There   c are   d There   e are
2 a is
3 a **There are** two keys on the table
  b **There are** three notebooks in my bag
  c There **is** a charger in the office
  d There **are** two cars on the street
  e **There's** an umbrella in my car
4 There are five desks in the classroom
  There are ten chairs in the classroom
  There's a bag on the table
  There's a textbook on the table
5 1, 2, 2, 1, 2

4.2
1 No! Jupiter is there!
  We are here. This is Earth.
  Look, Lurian! What are those?
  They're cars.
  Oh, no! What's that?
2 a these, They   b This, It
  c these, they, They d this, it
3 b It's **a** charger   c It's an umbrella
  d **They're** my keys e What are **these**?
  f What **are** these?
4 This, These, that, father, those, brothers, That, are
5 a green   b gray   c white   d black
  e yellow f blue   g brown   h orange
  i pink   j red

4.3
1 /ɪz/ sunglasses, watches
2 a cell phone   b rings   c candies
  d sunglasses e backpack f watches
3 Personal answers.
4 a There **are** two bananas on the table.
  b My **notebook** is in my backpack **or**
    My notebooks **are** in my backpack.
  c **Are there** tablets in the school?   d Correct.
  e **Are there** dictionaries in your classroom?
  f **Is there** a flash drive in your office?   g Correct.
  h **There is** an umbrella in my car.
  i **Are there** good soccer players in your school?
5 b Eleven twenty   e Eight thirty
  c Seven fifteen   f One ten
  d Nine fifty

4.4
1 1 c   2 e   3 a   4 b   5 d
2 1 get up   2 check your phone
  3 have breakfast   4 leave home
  5 have lunch   6 go to the gym
  7 have dinner   8 go to bed
3 2 She checks her phone at 6:05.
  3 She has breakfast at 6:15.
  4 She leaves home at 7 o'clock.
  5 She has lunch at 1 o'clock.
  6 She goes to the gym at 5:30.
  7 She has dinner at 6:20.
  8 She goes to bed at 10:15.
4 Personal answers

4.5
1 3, 1, 5, 2, 4
2 a Nine years old in 2020.
  b Three students.
  c Nearly 20 million.
  d No. Its original name was Picaboo.
3 1 Email   2 Facebook
  3 Blog   4 Smartphone
  5 Apps   6 Tweet
  7 Gigabyte   Secret word: Information

Unit 5

5.1
1 [word search grid]

2 a milk   b meat   c coffee
  d fruit   e vegetables f soft drinks
3 a beans   b fruit   c meat   d egg
4 orange juice   pancakes (b)   soup (d)
  croissants (a) chocolate   bread   butter (c)
  coffee   rice   fruit
5 a T   b F   c F   d T   e F
6 a What is your favorite meal? breakfast / lunch / dinner
  b Do you eat meat? Yes, I do. / No, I don't.
  c What do you have for lunch? Personal answer.
  d Is fruit good for you? Yes, it is.
  e Do you have bad habits? Yes, I do. / No, I don't.

5.2
1 a grapes   b beef   c orange   d pizza
  e carrot   f French fries   g lettuce
2 d bananas (1st column)   g chicken (2nd column)
  b fish (this is the food item that doesn't go in the
    columns, because it's a monosyllable)
  a hamburger (3rd column)   e kiwi (2nd column)
  f potatoes (1st column)   c tomatoes (1st column)
  h vegetables (3rd column)
3 b Do you like grapes?   c I don't like carrots.
  d Graeme hates fish.   e My dad loves bananas.
  f Does Phil like pasta? g Andrea doesn't like beef.
4 a John **likes** chicken very much.
  b They **don't** like fish.
  c She **doesn't** like hamburgers.
  d **Do** you like onions?
  e He doesn't **like** tomatoes.
5 Personal answers.

5.3
1 2 Monday   3 Tuesday   4 Wednesday
  5 Thursday   6 Friday   7 Saturday
2 a T   b T   c F   d F   e T
3 a Friday's my favorite day of the week.
  b I don't usually go to church on Sunday.
  c My partner hates Mondays.
  d I sometimes go to the gym on weekends.
  e My wife and I always go shopping together on
    Saturday.
  f We never watch TV in the evening.
4 Personal answers.
5 never, sometimes, usually, always
6 a I _____ read …   d I _____ go …
  b I _____ read …   e … I _____ listen …
  c I _____ buy …
7 a on   b in   c on   d in   e on

5.4
1 b Gabriel García Márquez's books are …
  c Leonardo da Vinci's inventions are …
  d Banksy's art is …
  e Jamie Oliver's food is …
  f Martin Scorsese's movies are …
2 d, a, c, b
3 a Van Gogh's   b Shakira's   c Harry Kane's
  d Lewis Hamilton's
4 a The White House is **the U.S. President's official
    residence.**
  b **Adele's songs** are beautiful.
  c **Shakira's son's name's** Milan.
  d Sunflowers is one of **Van Gogh's famous paintings**.
5 a him   b her   c them   d it
6 a What's your mother's name?
  b What's your partner's name?
  c What's your best friend's job?
  d Who's your favorite singer?
  e What's your favorite movie?
  f What do you think of Jessica Alba?
  Personal answers for the second part of the rubric.

5.5
1 French fries, cheeseburger, pizza, vanilla milkshake, hot
  dog, salad, chocolate ice cream, Coke.
2 **c**heeseburger, **F**rench fries, **C**oke, **p**izza, **s**alad, **h**ot
  dog, **v**anilla **m**ilkshake, **c**hocolate **i**ce **c**ream
3 a cream   b ice   c small   d pizza   e like
4 Personal answers.
5 d, c, b, a, e, h, f, g
6 1 a   2 b   3 a   4 b   5 b   6 a

117

Phrase Bank

This Phrase Bank is organized by topics.
○ The audio is on the ID Richmond Learning Platform, unit by unit.

Greetings
Unit 1
Hello.
Hi.
Nice to meet you.
Nice to meet you, too.
Good to see you.
How are you?
I'm fine, thanks.
Good morning / afternoon / evening / night.
Bye for now.
Bye!
Goodbye.
See you.

Classroom language
Unit 1
Listen to the dialogue.
Listen and repeat.
Look at the photos.
No phones in class.
One moment, please.
Please help me!
Practice the sentences.
Read the text.
Sorry?
Speak English, OK?
Spell that, please.
Thanks!
You're welcome!
Welcome to the New ID School of English.
Work in pairs.

Talking about people and things
Unit 1
Please! What's this? A pen?
No, it isn't a pen. It's a pencil!
I don't know.
This is my friend Javier.
What's this in English, please?
What do you call this?
It's a notebook.

Unit 2
Who's Hugh Jackman?
He's an actor.
What's a BMW?
It's a car.

Unit 4
Are those your books?
How many students are there in this class?
Only one.
There are a lot of students.
What are these in English?

Personal information
Unit 1
Are you married?
No, I'm single.
I'm Isadora Torres.
My name is Luiza.
Please, call me Dora.
What's your name?
What's your phone number?
Are you on WhatsApp?
What's your email address?
Where are you from?
I'm from Salvador.

Unit 2
Are you Puerto Rican / from Puerto Rico?
How old are you?
I'm 19 (years old).
How old is he?
He's 22 (years old).
He's around 30.
Is he married?
No, he's single.
Where is he from?
He's from Spain.

Unit 3
Do you have children?
Yes, I do. I have a son.
Do you live alone?
No, I don't. I live with my grandmother.
Do you live near here?
No, I live downtown.
Here's my number.

Asking for confirmation
Unit 2
Are you sure?
I'm not sure.
I don't know.
(I have) No idea.

Opinions
Unit 2
Who's your favorite actor?
What's your favorite movie?
Ariana Grande is an incredible musician.
I agree. She's fantastic!
Fortnite is a terrible video game.
I disagree. I think it's good.

Unit 4
I (don't) think people are honest here.
I think it's the same here.
It depends.

Unit 5
Moderation is good.
I agree.

Phrase Bank

I disagree.
What do you think of Adele?
I don't like her.
I love her.

Jobs
Unit 3
Do you work at home?
His parents are retired.
What do you do?
I'm a doctor.
I'm unemployed.
What do you want to be?
I want to be a lawyer.
Where do you want to work?
I want to work at home.
Where do you work?
I work in a factory.
Where does your mother work?

Family
Unit 3
Do you have children?
Yes, I do. Two daughters.
Do you have brothers and sisters?
I have two brothers.
I have two siblings: Lucy and Jack.
Does she have a sister?
I'm an only child.
Is he your husband?
My family is big.
I have a lot of relatives.
Meghan is married to Harry.

Showing interest
Unit 3
All right!
Cool!
Great talking to you.
Nice.
Oh, I see.
Really?
Wow!

Food
Unit 5
Do you drink a lot of coffee?
Do you eat a lot of fast food?
Do you eat meat?
Do you like Chinese food?
Not really, but I like Indian.
Do you like grapes?
I don't like grapes.
I prefer wine!
Do you like vegetables?
I don't like vegetables, but I eat them because they're good for me.

I like chicken very much.
I love dinner. It's my favorite meal.
What do you have for lunch?
Soft drinks are bad for you.
What kind of food do you like?
What kind of fruit does your brother like?
He likes oranges.
What's your favorite food?
I'm terrible. I really like fast food!

At a restaurant
Unit 3
Another soda?

Unit 5
Anything else?
Anything to eat?
Anything to drink?
A cola, please.
Can I help you?
Cream or sugar?
For here or to go?
For here. / To go.
Large, medium, or small?
With ice?
That's $12.95.
There you are. Thanks a lot.

Weekend activities
Unit 5
I don't go to the gym on Saturday.
In the afternoons we play video games.
We sometimes go to a bar in the evening.
My friends and I never stay home on Saturday night.
We sometimes go to a restaurant.
I go to the movies on weekends.
We always play soccer on Friday.
What do you do on Saturdays?
What do you usually do on the weekend?
I play soccer or baseball on Sunday mornings.

Other useful expressions
Unit 1
I love English.
No smoking.
Sorry. I don't remember.

Unit 2
What year is it?
I need English for my job.
What's the opposite of hot?

Unit 4
How do you pronounce *meme* in English?

Unit 5
Is this your brother's name?
No, it's my son's name.
What about you?

119

Word List

This is a reference list. The audio is on the Richmond Learning Platform.

Unit 1

Numbers 1–12
1 one
2 two
3 three
4 four
5 five
6 six
7 seven
8 eight
9 nine
10 ten
11 eleven
12 twelve

Classroom items
a book
a chair
a desk
a flash drive
an eraser
an interactive whiteboard
a marker
a notebook
an online dictionary
a pen
a pencil
a tablet

Other vocabulary
banana
car
cat
mouse
phone

Unit 2

Famous people and things
actor
celebrity
movie
musician
politician
soccer player
song
video game

Opinion adjectives
bad
excellent
fantastic
good
horrible
incredible
OK
terrible

Countries
Brazil
China
Mexico
Spain
the UK
the U.S.
Venezuela

Nationalities
American
Brazilian
British
Canadian
Chinese
German
Italian
Japanese
Mexican
South Korean
Spanish
Venezuelan

Numbers 13–2000
13 thirteen
14 fourteen
15 fifteen
16 sixteen
17 seventeen
18 eighteen
19 nineteen
20 twenty
21 twenty-one
22 twenty-two
23 twenty-three
30 thirty
31 thirty-one
32 thirty-two
40 forty
41 forty-one
50 fifty
60 sixty
70 seventy
80 eighty
90 ninety
100 one hundred
101 one hundred one
111 one hundred eleven
121 one hundred twenty-one
1000 one thousand
2000 two thousand

Marital status
married
single

Other vocabulary
apartment
birthday
channel
dollar
kilo
kilometer
liter
miles per hour

Unit 3

Jobs
an actor
an architect
a bank cashier
a chef
a dentist
a doctor
an engineer
a hairdresser
an IT professional
a lawyer
a manager
a movie director
a musician
a nurse
an office worker
a painter
a pharmacist
a police officer
a programmer
retired
a sales clerk
a server
a soccer player
a taxi driver
a teacher
a travel agent
unemployed
a university professor
a writer

Family members
brother
children
couple
daughter
father
grandfather
grandmother
grandparents
husband
mother
parents
partner
siblings
sister
son
wife

Places of work
a bank
downtown
a drugstore
a factory
home
a hospital
an office
a restaurant
a school
a store
a travel agency

Unit 4

Personal items
a backpack
a bag
a camera
candies
a charger
a coin
a comb
headphones
an ID card
keys
a lipstick
make-up
mints
pills
sunglasses
an umbrella
a wallet
a watch

Other vocabulary
ball
box
photo

Unit 5

Meals
breakfast
dinner
lunch
snack

Food and drinks
apples
beans
beef
bread
carrots
cheese
cheeseburger
chicken
Chinese food
coffee
eggs
fish
French fries
fruit
grapes
hot dog
ice cream
Italian food
Japanese food
juice
kiwi
lettuce
meat
milk
milkshake
orange
pizza
potatoes
rice
salad
soft drinks
sugar
tea
tomatoes
vegetables
wine

Weekend activities
cook
cycling
go to church
go to a restaurant
go to the gym
go to the mall
go to the movies
listen to music
play soccer / baseball
play video games
read a book
see friends
swimming
take a dance class
watch TV

Days of the week
Sunday
Monday
Tuesday
Wednesday
Thursday
Friday
Saturday

Frequency adverbs
always
usually
sometimes
never

Places to eat
café
restaurant